INTERMEDIATE LOAN

THIS ITEM MAY BE BORROWE

ONE WEEK ON

INTERMEDIATE LOANS ARE IN HEA
PLEASE RETURN OR REN

To renew, telephone:
01243 816089 (B
01243 812

D0531698

Effective Intervention in Primary Schools: Nurture Groups

Second Edition

Marion Bennathan
and Marjorie Boxall

 **David Fulton** Publishers

WS 2317147 2

12.2010

All royalties from this book go to promote the
work of Nurture Groups with the support of the AWCEBD,
of Charlton Court, East Sutton, Kent ME17 3DQ.
Registered Charity Number 258730

This edition reprinted 2008 by Routledge
2 Park Square, Milton Park, Abingdon, Oxon, OX14 4RN
Simultaneously published in the USA and Canada by Routledge
270 Madison Avenue, New York, NY 10016

UNIVERSITY OF CHICHESTER

First published in Great Britain by David Fulton Publishers 1996
Second edition 2002, reprinted 2001, 2003, 2004, 2005 and 2008
10 9 8 7 6

Note: The right of Marion Bennathan and Marjorie Boxall to be identified as
the authors of this work has been asserted by them in accordance with the
Copyright, Designs and Patents Act 1988.

Copyright © Marion Bennathan and Marjorie Boxall 2000

British Library Cataloguing in Publication Data
A catalogue record for this book is available from the British Library.

ISBN 1 85346 706 5

All rights reserved. No part of this publication may be reproduced, stored in a
retrieval system or transmitted, in any form, or by any means, electronic,
mechanical, photocopying, recording or otherwise, without the prior
permission of the publishers.

Typeset by FiSH Books, London
Printed and bound in Great Britain

370.
904
BEN

Contents

Foreword

I am very pleased to have the chance to re-introduce this book to a wide audience of teachers and those involved in the education of teachers and in policy-making. Nurture groups are spreading rapidly throughout the UK. This fully updated second edition is written in response to the support given by the DfEE to the Nurture Group project and the recognition by every major special needs policy document that they provide effective early intervention for children showing signs of emotional and behavioural difficulties.

We are coming to an even clearer recognition than before that children's deprivation, including not only economic deprivation but, more crucially still, emotional, linguistic and intellectual deprivation, leads to educational failure. Yet the sad pattern of learning difficulties, increasingly anti-social or violent behaviour, truancy or exclusion and delinquency, is not inevitable. Teachers can in many cases compensate for deprivation and can prepare children for school in such a way that they can learn to succeed. And the earlier this intervention comes the better. At last we are seeing a slow recognition that early education of a structured kind with properly trained teachers is the only way ahead if we want to prevent not just crime but criminality.

And we should have a greater vision. We should hope more than anything that we can introduce all children to the pleasure of reasonable self-esteem, of conversation, of ambitions achieved, to the pleasures, in short, that education brings. No child should be deprived of the chance of these benefits not only for the sake of keeping them out of prison but because they are worth having in themselves. We must catch children young if we are to introduce them to the values that will give meaning to their lives. Teachers have a tremendous responsibility here, and I hope that, reading this book, they will appreciate the great influence their teaching can have on children's lives and will feel encouraged to commit themselves to that responsibility as set out by the authors.

Mary Warnock
January 1996 and July 2000

Preface

The 1993 Education Act and the 1994 Code of Practice aimed to educate children in mainstream school wherever possible, to identify the special educational needs of all those at risk of failure, and to provide effective help. The children who challenge their teachers most because of their number and because of the range and complexity of their needs are those with emotional and behavioural difficulties. In the 1960s and '70s inner-city schools were similarly troubled and Marjorie Boxall, an educational psychologist in the Inner London Education Authority (ILEA) working with primary school teachers in North London, developed small special classes called 'nurture groups'. These were for children who came into school from harsh social circumstances showing all the signs of having missed out on essential early learning experiences.

The groups achieved dramatic change for the children placed in them; and, because acceptance by all the teachers in the school was a necessary condition, support for each other became part of the school ethos: a whole-school approach ensued. The groups were also very well-liked by parents who were often only too aware that their children needed extra help but resisted the idea of special school. (The term 'nurture group' was intended as an administrative name and caught on because it so exactly described the work of the groups. But schools avoided any possible offence to parents by always giving the groups a neutral name.) By the end of the 1970s some 50 schools were taking part in the project and nurture groups were singled out for praise by the Warnock Committee.

Marjorie Boxall was central to the work throughout, stimulating and supporting teachers, encouraging monitoring and evaluation, and developing with them diagnostic materials which enhanced teachers' understanding and the effectiveness of their intervention. The work of the nurture groups became widely known by lectures and conferences and by word of mouth. A large archive of records, videos and other training material was built up, two major evaluations exist, but the only significant publication was the pamphlet published in 1976, *The Nurture Group in the*

Primary School. This became unobtainable when ILEA was abolished in 1989.

The Association of Workers for Children with Emotional and Behavioural Difficulties (AWCEBD), whose chief aim is to improve provision for all children and young people with emotional and/or behavioural difficulties, valued the nurture group approach and were delighted when Marjorie Boxall agreed to the republication of the pamphlet, and when Baroness Warnock agreed to write a preface. But more was needed: a publication that made clear the relevance of the nurture group approach to the changed educational circumstances of the 1990s and which put it in a wider context of educational thinking. As Chair of the AWCEBD and as a close friend of Marjorie Boxall since we trained together as educational psychologists in 1956–7, I was the obvious person for this task. Chapter 2 of this book is essentially Marjorie Boxall's pamphlet. She also commented helpfully on the other four chapters, which were written by me, except for the section in Chapter 3, 'The Newcastle experience', which was written by Keith Hibbert, Mary McDonald, Willie Muir and David Simpson of the Newcastle upon Tyne Education Department, whose contribution is gratefully acknowledged.

I also record with thanks the contribution of former ILEA staff members, Liz Doak and Peggy Hall, Betty Hagestadt, Annie Henriques and Miriam Roberts. I am grateful to Enfield Education Department for allowing me to use material from their schools; to Evelyn Dixon, Eva Holmes, Joyce Iszatt and Pam King who all gave valuable information and support; I was also helped by Eve Boyd, Sue Burgess, Kay Eccles, Chris Eglington, Sandra Jordan, Linda Levi, Janice McGrath, Denise Nolan, Cathy Oakes-Monger, Miriam Perrin, Sue Simpson, Hazel Stockman and Jenny Wilder-Ahmed. I record thanks to Edith Biggs, HMI, to Peter Hodgson and Jo Richardson of the Caldecott Community, to Tim Smith and other staff of Warleigh Manor, to Paul Cooper, Sue Panter, Allan Rimmer, Jacquie Wicks and other members of the AWCEBD.

The support over many years of Randolph Boxall and Esra Bennathan is gratefully recorded, and I thank Joss, Joel, Ella, Matthias, Rosa and Oliver Bennathan for the education they continue to provide for me, as well as the love and joy.

Marion Bennathan
March 1996 and July 2000

Introduction to the Second Edition

Since the first edition of this book appeared in 1996 there have been developments in government policies in the United Kingdom which make effective early intervention and therefore nurture groups ever more relevant. The new administration coming into power in May 1997 had by July brought out their statement of aims for all state schools, *Excellence in Schools* (DfEE, 1997a) which committed the government to achieving higher attainments for all children. Closely defined prescriptive policies followed: the introduction of a 'literacy hour' and a 'numeracy hour' in all primary schools; the setting of academic targets to be met in the national tests and examinations at various stages; the publication of schools' results with radical action to be taken when schools were seen as failing their pupils. All this was set in a policy of inclusion, that is that the great majority of children, whatever their disability, were to be educated in mainstream school.

AWCEBD and the DfEE

It was clear to the Association of Workers for Children with Emotional and Behavioural Difficulties (AWCEBD) that the pressure to raise standards, however desirable, would do nothing to make children with emotional and behavioural difficulties welcome in mainstream schools. Nor would their presence there do much to help well-functioning children to make the good progress demanded. The Association therefore drew the attention of the Secretary of State for Education to the relevance of nurture groups to many aspects of government policy, to reducing exclusions, to raising academic standards, to increasing social inclusion by reducing truancy and improving behaviour. This resulted in official support for nurture groups in all the major policy documents on special educational needs.

Excellence for All Children: Meeting Special Educational Needs

A second policy paper *Excellence for All Children: Meeting Special Educational Needs* (DfEE, 1997b) quickly followed *Excellence in Schools*.

This states that the government's 'vision is of excellence for all. This inclusive vision encompasses children with special educational needs.' The paper for the first seven of its eight chapters addresses itself to questions of principle and practice for all children with special educational needs (SEN). The only children given a chapter to themselves are the 'one group which presents schools with special challenges – children with emotional and behavioural difficulties. The number of children perceived as falling within this group is increasing.' (op.cit., p. 77).

One of the principles stressed is that of early identification and intervention, with nurture groups in Enfield cited as *the* example of good practice:

Nurture groups in Enfield
In Enfield, some primary schools run nurture groups for children showing early signs of emotional and behavioural difficulties. These small special classes provide a structured and predictable environment in which the children can begin to trust adult and to learn. Careful consideration is given to appropriate curriculum content. The nurture groups are an integral part of Enfield schools' mainstream provision for children with special educational needs. The LEA's advisory staff and educational psychology service support and train the nurture group teachers and assistants.

Parents are regularly involved in discussion about their child's progress and attend informal sessions. Pupils are encouraged to take part in school activities including assemblies and playtimes. Many pupils are able to function wholly within a mainstream class within a year.

Excellence for all Children was put out for consultation and evoked an unusually large response, from 3,600 groups and individuals, much of it favourable. What attracted most criticism was the inclusion of children with EBD. ('A recipe for disaster' was the comment of the leader of one teachers' union.) To consider the response and to draw up plans for implementing the policy, the DfEE set up a National Advisory Group on Special Educational Needs, whose sub-group on EBD included Marion Bennathan.

A Programme of Action

The publication which resulted, *Meeting Special Educational Needs: A Programme of Action* (DfEE, 1998), addressed the themes of *Excellence for All Children*, describing how the aims set out there would be achieved. On emotional and behavioural difficulties, it was written that all Local Education Authorities (LEAs) were required to have 'a statement of their arrangements for dealing with their pupils' behavioural difficulties. Plans must include information on the advice and resources available to schools for promoting good behaviour and discipline and dealing with pupils with behaviour problems'.

It was also announced (p. 44) that:

A national programme will be in place to help primary schools tackle emotional and behavioural difficulties at an early stage.

Primary nurture groups – we are supporting, in partnership with the University of Cambridge and the Association of Workers for Children with Emotional and Behavioural Difficulties, a research project to promote primary age nurture groups for children who on entry to school show the effects of inadequate early learning experiences. They offer an educational programme precisely structured to the emotional, social and intellectual needs of each pupil while keeping them in close contact with their normal class.

Social Inclusion: Pupil Support

Next, as part of the drive to raise attainments for all children, the government addressed the need for all agencies working with children to work together to prevent children becoming excluded from society. The paper *Social Inclusion: Pupil Support* was produced by the DfEE in collaboration with the Social Exclusion Unit (part of the Cabinet Office and central to a wide range of government policies), with the Home Office and with the Department of Health. It focused particularly on the need for regular attendance at school and high standards of behaviour; on reducing the level of unauthorized absences and exclusions. It acknowledged that some pupils are at particular risk of poor attendance or of exclusion, notably those with emotional and/or behavioural difficulties. It makes clear that efforts to help pupils to progress in mainstream school 'should be seen in the context of wider action, nationally and locally, to prevent social exclusion – supporting local communities, encouraging employment and reducing crime'.

Again, attention was drawn to the effective early intervention provided by nurture groups, the example given (p.11) being the group at Raynham School in Enfield:

Aim: to use small Nurture Groups for children showing early signs of emotional and behavioural difficulties

Many of the children entering the school have a history of disrupted parenting and seriously under-developed social and linguistic skills that make participation in mainstream learning difficult. The small special classes provide a structured and predictable environment in which children can begin to trust adults and to learn.

Pupils from reception to Year 2 begin their day with their mainstream class and return for story time at the end. They are encouraged to take part in assemblies and playtimes. They spend the rest of their time in a small separate classroom following a carefully chosen curriculum including activities to develop social skills and confidence to take part in mainstream classes within 3–5 terms.

Nurture groups are an integral part of Enfield's mainstream provision for children with special educational needs. The educational psychologists and the LEA advisory staff support and train staff. Parents are involved in their children's progress and attend informal sessions.

The spread of nurture groups

Clearly, the concept of effective early intervention has considerable appeal at a time of great concern about educational standards and about the dangers, immediate and long-term, of social exclusion as was recognized in reactions to the first edition of this book. Ron Davie, for example, formerly Director of the National Children's Bureau, described it in a review article in the *Times Educational Supplement* (20 September 1996) as:

> a seminal new book [which] should be read by all education ministers and their shadows . . . by all who are concerned about the increasing incidence of behaviour problems in our schools and about the significant and worrying escalation in the number of pupils excluded in recent years. The implications for schools are serious enough. The implications for society of a growing number of alienated young people with little or no adequate alternative educational provision, at risk of drifting into a life of crime or drugs, or both, are frightening.

With such encouragement, a small group experienced in nurture group work began to offer day conferences to anyone interested in learning more about the groups. The response from those attending, largely educationists, was extremely positive. They immediately understood the significance of what we had to tell them. Many of them wanted to know how to set up nurture groups; we were urged to tell the world, in particular the government, of what they could achieve. As will be evident from the support of the DfEE described above, we followed their advice.

With government endorsement, the demand for information and training in nurture group work grew. It was clear that more people were needed to help. Early in 1998 the AWCEBD therefore set up a sub-committee, the Nurture Group Consortium, to take the work forward. In September 1998, the University of Cambridge School of Education agreed to set up the Nurture Group Project under the direction of Dr Paul Cooper, to promote and research nurture groups. The Project was extremely fortunate to be able to secure the services of Ray Arnold and Eve Boyd, until recently senior advisers in Enfield LEA, both with experience of nurture groups. As well as the financial support offered by the DfEE in its *Programme of Action* the Calouste Gulbenkian Foundation and the University of Cambridge made contributions.

The Project now offers a Certificate in the Theory and Practice of Nurture Group Work which at the time of writing has attracted some 200 applicants. Most of these are teachers, some are learning support assistants, some educational psychologists. The course runs two two-day sessions separated by a month to allow time for a child study to be carried out and students' evaluations are uniformly positive, indeed enthusiastic. The Project works closely with the Nurture Group Consortium, most of whose members contribute to the teaching on the Certificate Course. In addition the Consortium offers training at many other levels, such as workshops, lectures and day conferences.

As well as training, the Cambridge Project is concerned with researching the effect of nurture groups. Its first Report *The Nature and Distribution of Nurture Groups in England and Wales* (Cooper, Arnold and Boyd, 1999) was completed in October 1999.

It became clear when a further reprinting of the original *Effective Intervention in Primary Schools: Nurture Groups* was planned that so much had happened in the last four years that a completely new edition was required. There was much progress to be reported; the rapid spread of nurture groups is gratifying. But sudden fame has its dangers, and problems of definition – of quality assurance – have arisen which need to be addressed. The result is this revised edition with a new final chapter which looks at these issues. The rest of the book remains substantially as in the first edition.

I should like to dedicate this new edition to those who work with the Nurture Group Consortium and whose undiminished enthusiasm carries the work forward. As well as the members of the Cambridge Project, named above, they are Eva Holmes, Joyce Iszatt, Pam King, Sylvia Lucas, Jim Parker, Jo Richardson, Allan Rimmer and, above all, Marjorie Boxall, without whom there would be no nurture groups.

On a personal note, I thank Clara Bennathan, born in December 1996, for the delight of her enthusiastic comments on life as she understands it.

Marion Bennathan
June 2000

Chapter 1

Children at Risk of Failure in Primary Schools

Marion Bennathan

Many young children in our schools cause great concern: they fail to make progress in their learning; they may behave badly so that they spoil their own educational chances and those of the rest of their class; they may be depressed, withdrawn, self-destructive. They evoke stress, uncertainty, even guilt in their teachers whose management skills they challenge beyond reasonable limits. Their failure to benefit from their time in school is likely to have serious consequences for their own life chances. It will also have consequences for the rest of society in their inability to make satisfactory adult relationships and provide adequate parenting, their need for welfare or mental health support, in rates of criminality.

It is difficult to know whether or not the number of children with emotional and behavioural difficulties in school is increasing. There are no agreed criteria for what constitutes a significant difficulty so that it is not possible to collect comprehensive data about incidence which would show changes over time. But the popular opinion, often reflected in the media, would certainly be that there is an increase of unacceptable behaviour as well as of distress in young people. This view is strongly supported by the authoritative work of Rutter and Smith (1995), *Psychosocial Disorders in Young People*, which records clear evidence from research over the last 50 years of massive increases in young people aged between 12 and 26 throughout Western Europe of reported criminality, substance abuse, depressive illnesses and suicides.

Exclusions

What has also increased sharply in the last few years is the number of children who have been excluded from mainstream school for unacceptable behaviour. There were already in 1991 widespread reports of rapid increases in the numbers of such children being excluded, of children as young as five being found too difficult for their teachers, of pressure on special resources (Bennathan, 1992). Parsons *et al.* (1994) in *Excluding Primary School*

Children reported that the Department for Education estimated the number of permanent exclusions in 1993/94 at between 7,000 and 8,000 compared with about 3,000 three years earlier, when exclusions were already reportedly much higher than before.

It is impossible to say whether this increase really represents more serious emotional and behavioural difficulties in children or whether it is due to a changed response in schools which, it is often suggested, might be caused by increased teacher stress because of the many changes and extra work resulting from the 1988 Education Act. It may also be that there is less tolerance of disruptive behaviour because of 'the impact of the National Curriculum on schools as heads and governors are forced to compete with each other and publish league tables of comparative performance', as the Association of Metropolitan Authorities (1995) writes in its report on special educational needs.

Whatever the increased pressures, there is no reason to believe that schools are excluding children without good reason. Parsons *et al.* (1994, p. 17) write, 'The evidence shows that the teachers involved with these pupils worked hard to contain them and to teach them, along with all the other children in the class, for a considerable length of time before the possibility of exclusion arose.' Exclusion from school is clearly most undesirable; the failure to help such children adequately so that exclusion is avoided is serious in its consequences for them individually and it also has serious social implications. Those whose difficulties are emotional rather than behavioural are likely to be at greater risk of psychiatric illness in adult life as a result of rejection by their school. Those whose difficulties are behavioural pose a more obvious threat to society as well as to their own educational prospects, behaviour disorders in childhood having long been recognized as predictors of antisocial adult behaviour. (The evidence for this is comprehensively discussed in 'Youth Crime and Conduct Disorders', in Rutter and Smith, 1995.)

Parsons (Parsons *et al.* 1994, p. 7) points out that children expelled from school spend an average of nine months waiting for a new placement and may often wait a whole term before receiving any home tuition, which will then often be for only three hours a week. Excluded children are likely to come from homes that are already finding it difficult to provide adequate care and control for them even when they are attending school, so it is most unlikely that they will be able to provide a positive experience when they are at home all day long. Parsons' conclusion from his research is that 'the prospect of what these children might become, and what might happen to them, without appropriate provision, is frightening'. The AMA report likewise recognizes that 'Exclusions can represent the last departure point, typically for boys, before they become entrenched in an alternative culture of crime'.

Increased exclusions are only one indicator of the increased number of children showing emotional and behavioural difficulties in our schools. It may be assumed that for every child with difficulties extreme enough to warrant exclusion there will be several not quite at that point but still drastically failing to achieve adequate standards of work and behaviour and often also seriously affecting the progress of their classmates. The aim of our education system is to offer all children the best possible preparation for adult life; it is, therefore, a matter of urgency that as much as possible is done to prevent emotional and behavioural difficulties affecting the quality of life for everybody in school.

Emotional and behavioural difficulties as a special educational need

One way to tackle the problem is to classify a child presenting serious emotional or behavioural difficulties as having a learning disability. This approach goes back to the 1944 Education Act where 'maladjustment' was for the first time accepted as a category of disability requiring special education in some form, along with such well-recognized conditions as mental handicap and sensory and physical disabilities. Since the 1981 Education Act emotional and behavioural difficulties, if they are thought serious enough to affect a child's learning, constitute a 'special educational need' which may lead to a formal statement of entitlement to extra educational resources, a procedure which is no doubt essential for some children.

It would, however, be over simple to think that provision for children showing such difficulties is comparable with provision for other groups of children with special educational needs. There are considerable problems in comparing emotional and behavioural difficulties with such conditions as visual or hearing impairment, or other well-defined handicaps to good learning. A deaf child, for example, has a measurable hearing loss for which there is appropriate specialist teaching. Children either have impaired hearing or they do not; deafness is not dependent on emotional or social circumstances. It is a condition which is well understood, both medically and educationally.

Having 'emotional and behavioural difficulties' (EBD), by contrast, presents great problems of definition. All children are emotionally or behaviourally difficult sometimes; in a badly run class, many are so much of the time. The condition is not necessarily intrinsic to the child who, moved to a happier setting, might cease to have EBD. Also the causes of such difficulties are complex: some children live in difficult family circumstances, some are responding to distressing life events. In other words, having emotional and behavioural difficulties is not a clear-cut condition intrinsic to the child. The arguments in 1978 at the time of the influential Report, *Special Educational Needs* (DES, 1978; widely known as the Warnock Report, the precursor of the 1981 Education Act), against keeping the term 'maladjusted' were that it suggested a hard and fast condition. This thereby deflected attention from the circumstances that produced the undesirable behaviour, which might well include deficiencies in the management of such children in school.

Historically, individual differences in children had been seen as the main cause of differing educational progress, but the idea that individual differences in schools may be just as important is one that has been gaining ground over the last generation and is now centre stage. Rutter and colleagues (1979), in their landmark research, *Fifteen Thousand Hours: Secondary Schools and Their Effects on Children*, showed how schools with pupils from comparable backgrounds achieved widely varying educational outcomes. The Elton Report (DES, 1989), *Discipline in Schools*, also put the emphasis not on individual children and their circumstances but on the importance of creating a positive atmosphere in schools for all children and for their teachers.

This recognition makes it impossible to hold that all children who show EBD are a discrete group requiring special treatment. The situation is more complex than that, as is now officially recognized by central government, notably in the guidance which accompanied the 1993 Education Act. This Act and its Code of Practice (DfE, 1994c), which largely replaced the 1981 Education Act on children with special educational needs, was preceded by extensive consultation, detailed by Davie (1994), with all the agencies concerned with children in difficulties. The Department for Education circular, *The Education of Children with Emotional and Behavioural Difficulties* (DfE, 1994b), is an admirable survey of the present state of thinking about such children. Of EBD as a special educational need, it states, 'There is no absolute definition... The difficulties are genuine. But EBD is often engendered or worsened by the environment, including schools' or teachers' responses' (p. 4).

The clear implication of this is that if all schools were as good as they might be at managing children's emotions and behaviour the incidence of EBD as a special educational need would decline. This is not to say there would no longer be any such thing as a child with serious emotional or behavioural difficulties. Some children have been so affected by extremely adverse experiences in their early years that they need more skilled help than can be offered by even the best mainstream schools. But the dangers in rushing to categorize children as EBD need to be underlined.

First, the demand for special placement would be high, which goes against the well-accepted policy first stated by the Warnock Report and reinforced by the 1993 Act that, with few exceptions, children should have the opportunity of mainstream education as the best preparation for adult life. Secondly, special placement is extremely expensive, using resources for a few that might enhance educational standards for the many. Thirdly, and this is perhaps in the long run the most important caveat, children with EBD should not be seen as a race apart. The processes they have gone through to make them severely EBD are only at the extreme end of the developmental processes gone through by all children. As someone memorably if inelegantly said, 'Maladjusted children are just the same as other children, only more so'.

Understanding the processes that make a few children incontrovertibly 'EBD' helps to a greater awareness of the potential hazards for many more of the children in our schools. It can lead to an increased awareness of the emotional needs of all children, an understanding which ought to be part of the professional competence of all teachers.

Preventing educational failure by early identification

The Warnock Report brought about important changes in our thinking about children with handicaps to good learning. Underlying the insistence on looking at each child individually, rather than at the category of handicap, is the recognition of the many factors that influence the child as it develops. It is widely acknowledged that children may be born, for example, with a profound hearing loss but that in itself does not determine their educational future; with early identification and good intervention the educational effects of the deafness can be greatly reduced. It is less widely recognized that children may be born into circumstances which deny them the early experiences on which later educational progress depends. What needs to exist for such children is a system that acknowledges these complexities, that looks out for children with disabilities of whatever sort and then defines what they need educationally to progress. That schools can make a great difference to the life prospects of disadvantaged children should be seen as an extremely positive message for the education service.

The Warnock Report estimated that in addition to the 2 per cent of children with difficulties severe enough to warrant a 'statement' of special educational need, there were about 18 per cent of children in mainstream schools with special educational needs that should be identified and special help provided if educational failure was to be avoided. It enjoined school governors and teachers to set up stages of assessment for the identification, monitoring and adequate teaching of these children.

It would probably be agreed that the educational prospects of the 2 per cent were considerably improved by the 1981 Act, but there is no such confidence that this also happened for the 18 per cent. As Sir Malcolm Thornton (1994), Chairman of the House of Commons Education Committee, reviewing legislation in education, wrote:

> The 1981 Act achieved significant change, particularly for the 2% of children needing special provision. It had, however, come at a time of pressure on LEA finances and had not had the impact hoped for on all schools. In particular it had not greatly improved the educational prospects of the 18% of children in mainstream schools estimated to have special educational needs at some point in their school lives. Visiting inner-city schools, it was clear that not all children were getting effective help.

The impact of the 1988 Education Act

Such help as these children were likely to get is generally acknowledged to have been threatened by the 1988 Education Reform Act. This, with its emphasis on raising academic standards and on making schools publicly accountable for their pupils' progress, had, to quote Thornton again, 'the unintended side effect of making schools less tolerant of children who needed more than their share of attention, particularly the group with emotional and behavioural difficulties'. Her Majesty's Inspectors, in their report for 1991–2, likewise noted the 'rising number of exclusions for pupils with emotional and behavioural difficulties in some Local Education Authorities' and further that 'few of those LEAs had evolved coherent strategies for managing the increase'.

Children at risk

Concern about what is seen as the increasing failure of the education system to help socially disadvantaged children is not only about their educational progress. There is growing disquiet, given frequent expression in the media, of a sizeable group of children and young people out of their parents' control, growing up apparently without moral standards, beyond the law, a danger to themselves and to others and likely to be a burden to society throughout their lives. Calls for action came to a crescendo in 1993 during the trial of two boys, aged 10 and 11, for the appalling murder of two-year-old James Bulger whom they had first abducted and tortured. The fact that both boys were out of school at the time of the murder and in severe difficulties with their education was noted. It was not unreasonable to fear that, as the number of children out of school was growing, other such crimes might be in the making.

In summer 1995, the Metropolitan Police Commissioner, launching a new campaign against street robbery, said: 'It is a fact that very many of the perpetrators of mugging are very young black people, who have been excluded from school.' In the heated public debate that followed, controversy centred on whether or not it was proper, fair or politic to single out one ethnic group. It would have been more constructive, the statement having been made, if those concerned for the welfare of our children had looked at the reality of life for young people who are rejected by their schools.

It has been known for some time that black adolescent boys are much more likely than white boys to be excluded by their schools. The Director of Education for the London Borough of Islington, for example, reported in 1992 (*Evening Standard*, 14 May, p. 14) an exclusion rate for black boys twice as high as for white boys and six times as high as for girls. Parsons *et al.* (1994, p. 7) writes that 'a number of authors have signalled race as a factor in exclusions'. This aspect of the problem was almost totally ignored in the media debate, and serious public discussion of it is long overdue.

The 1993 Education Act

The 1933 Education Act may be seen as trying to soften the impact of the 1988 Education Act on a large group of vulnerable children. Its Code of Practice offers the structures that can help schools to do better for such children. The stages of assessment, the careful monitoring of progress, the involvement of parents could, if enthusiastically followed, make a great difference to the life chances of many of our children. But if schools are to implement the Code with the seriousness it deserves, to allocate resources to children identified at an early stage in their school careers as having special educational needs, they must feel that successful intervention is within their reach. If they are to commit themselves wholeheartedly to the task, they must realize the great importance of what they can do and for that they need a realistic concept of child development and of precisely how adverse social circumstances affect educational progress.

We have been here before

A generation ago, there was similar concern about the increasing failure of mainstream schools to manage children with difficulties. The number of children being viewed as 'educationally subnormal' and put forward for special educational help was escalating rapidly. It was indeed one of the reasons for the setting up of the Warnock Committee in 1976. The Report stated:

The number of children in special schools had nearly doubled between 1947 and 1955 (from 12,060 to 22,639) yet the number of children awaiting placement remained high at over 12,000...Indeed, a special enquiry in 1956 showed that...as many as 27,000 were considered to need such placement. These were children who were not being satisfactorily helped in ordinary schools. (2.54)

This was particularly the case in inner-city areas. Studies carried out, for example, on 10-year-old children in one London Borough in 1970 showed high rates of behavioural difficulties, psychiatric disorder and reading retardation. The study reported by Rutter and colleagues (1975) found that teachers rated 19.1 per cent of their pupils to have 'behavioural deviance' which compared with 10.6 per cent in the Isle of Wight study (Rutter *et al.*, 1970). On the basis of interviews with parents, 25.4 per cent of children were found to be showing signs of psychiatric disorder compared with 12 per cent in the Isle of Wight. The London study was replicated by the ILEA Research Unit over the whole of Inner London with similar results (DES, 1978, 3.12).

Nurture groups: an innovative approach

Faced with the reality reflected in the statistics, and with referrals coming in at an overwhelming rate, Marjorie Boxall, an educational psychologist employed by the Inner London Education Authority (ILEA) in Hackney, an area of North London ranking high on all indices of social deprivation, felt that change was needed. If so many children could not adjust to school then the schools must re-examine their management of the children. With support from the child guidance clinic where she was based, from her teacher colleagues and from ILEA, she established the first experimental 'nurture groups', one in an infant school and one in a junior school, in 1970–71.

Nurture groups were special classes of some 12 children in primary schools run by a teacher and a helper. They were for children already in the school who were showing signs of severely deprived early childhoods, unable to learn because of extreme withdrawal or disruptiveness. For some children, 'everything that could go wrong had gone wrong', and it seemed that the only thing to do with them was to start again. This meant recreating in school the total experience of a normally developing child from babyhood onwards. The routine of the nurture group day was planned to provide a predictable, reliable structure in which the children would come to feel safe and cared for, so that they began to trust the adults, to explore and to learn. The structure combined the nurturing of an adequate family with the control required to manage in a group, taking turns, waiting, making choices, carrying tasks through to completion and clearing away. The children then began to make sense of their experiences, to be able to ask questions, to discuss, to feel some control over their environment and to internalize some control over their behaviour.

It was essential that the teacher and helper worked together, demonstrating considerate and cooperative behaviour, supporting each other, sharing, discussing, occasionally disagreeing and resolving their differences politely and responsibly; generally providing a model of positive adult behaviour, in control but responsive to the children's needs.

The groups were an integral part of the school, the children maintaining daily contact with their base class, so that the support and understanding of all the school staff was needed. This meant that whole-school preparation was needed before a group could be set up, which in itself proved to be a valuable exercise in spreading an understanding of the developmental processes underlying good educational progress and in creating a positive school ethos. The groups were quickly so successful that by 1978 the Warnock Committee could report:

> Among compensatory measures which may be taken we have been impressed by the 'nurture groups' which have been started in a number of primary schools in London for children approaching or over the age of five who are socially and emotionally affected by severe deprivation in early childhood. We believe that children under school age who are suffering from the same effects of severe deprivation could also benefit from this specific, intensive kind of help. (DES, 1978, 5.30)

The principle underlying the groups was that of responding to each child at whatever developmental age or stage he or she might be; whether needing comfort like a baby, control like a two-year-old in a tantrum, attention like a three-year-old who asks endless questions apparently for the sake of asking questions, or a four-year-old making grandiose claims not well based on reality. As the children's needs were reliably met, not ignored or rebuffed as they would have had to be in a normal class if indeed they could have been expressed there, the children developed greater trust and self-confidence, became better organized and were ready for formal learning.

Early learning

What the nurture groups were doing, implicitly, was to translate the growing understanding of early developmental processes into educational practice. This understanding had two main sources: ethology – the study of animal behaviour – and child psychiatry, the former having the advantage over the latter that it can for research purposes vary quite radically the conditions in which the young of the species are reared. Harlow, for example, studied rhesus monkeys reared in social isolation and showed devastating effects on their later social relationships (Harlow and Harlow, 1972). Earlier, Konrad Lorenz, one of the founders of ethology, had drawn attention to 'imprinting' or bonding processes in his charming, best-selling book *King Solomon's Ring* (Lorenz, 1952). In this he described the complex and in-built processes by which the young attach themselves to their parent; famously, how he managed to give a clutch of ducklings as they hatched the signals which convinced them that he was their mother, so that they trustingly followed him around in a line.

The second, and, for our purposes, more important influence was the work of child psychologists and psychiatrists, of whom the foremost was John Bowlby. In 1944, he published 'Forty-four Juvenile Thieves: Their Characters and Home Life' which made the connection between the lack of consistent and caring relationships in early childhood and later development. Later, he was much influenced by the work of Lorenz which stimulated his interest in the precise nature of the mother–baby interactions. His work was carried forward by Mary Ainsworth, a research psychologist, who tested Bowlby's theories by setting up a 'Strange Situation' laboratory in which babies and their mothers were studied. The baby's behaviour was observed when the mother was present, when the child was left alone with a strange woman (the researcher) and when the mother reappeared.

Ainsworth's observations led her to classify the child's attachment to the mother as (a) secure, (b) avoidant or (c) ambivalent or resistive. She concluded that the infant's behaviour was a good marker of the kind of care-giving experienced in the first year of life. The children classed as 'secure' – by far the largest number:

> used their mothers as a clear basis for exploration – that is they explored freely in her presence, checked on her whereabouts periodically, restricted exploration in her absence, showed varying levels of distress in her absence ranging from simple inhibition of play/exploration to extreme distress, but all greeted her positively on her return.

The next most common pattern was labelled 'avoidant' – 'infants appeared to explore without interest in their mothers' whereabouts, were minimally distressed by her departure, and appeared to snub or ignore her when she returned'. Children classified as ambivalent/resistive were shown to have a less harmonious relationship with their mothers at home than the other groups (Ainsworth *et al.*, 1978).

Changing practice

In most fields of work with children, the crucial importance of these early experiences and their influence on later behaviour was becoming widely accepted by the late 1950s. For example, the publication by the World Health Organisation of Bowlby's *Maternal Care and Child Health* (Bowlby, 1951), which drew attention to the dangers to the child's development of prolonged separation from the mother, began slowly to lead to changes in hospital practice. Until then, parents were not allowed to visit their babies and small children in hospital on the grounds that they were distressed when the parents departed.

Slowly, it became accepted that small children needed to have their mother or other significant adult with them throughout their stay. In social work there were similar widespread changes in practice, with much more attention given to the central relationship of parent and child, the avoidance of separation where possible and, if not, the keeping of contact by whatever means available. Although there were criticisms of Bowlby's hypotheses when they first appeared, both from psychoanalytic circles and from very different schools of thought, they have by now gained wide acceptance in most areas of work to do with children. Earlier ideas of the child as a passive recipient of parental care have been replaced by that of the child as a vigorous partner with his or her own influential perceptions of the relationship.

The scientific study of early childhood is now well established. It is accepted that babies quickly attach themselves emotionally to their adult carers and go through well-recognized stages of development towards maturity. Moving on well to the next stage depends on needs having been adequately met at the earlier stage. It can be shown, for example, that very young babies try to evoke visual, vocal and tactile responses and that if these are not forthcoming they show signs of distress. If the deprivation is severe enough, their attempts to make contact with their adult carer diminish and development is impaired.

> Unless there is skilful intervention they will persist in inappropriate attachment behaviour, whether over-anxious, or avoidant and aggressive, or will become quite incapable of warm attachment and therefore indifferent to human relationships. (Harris-Hendriks and Figueroa, 1995)

In education, however, the public service that affects all children, there was no comparable explicit recognition of this changed understanding of early experience and its crucial influence on later outcomes. The 1989 Children Act and the 1988 Education Act were simultaneously going through lengthy processes of preparation and consultation. Implicit in the first is the belief that children have a point of view, that their views and perceptions must be taken into account if their cooperation is expected when plans are being made for their future. There was nothing in the Education Act to acknowledge the child's point of view. There was and still is in much educational thinking the assumption that children come into school with more or less similar experiences and attitudes. It is not fully recognized that children have widely and crucially differing pre-school experiences and very different opportunities to acquire intellectual and social skills. They therefore start their formal education at different stages of development not because of their innate endowment but because of what has or has not happened to them. From this lack of awareness of the importance of early experience it is an easy step to assume that the child who cannot cope with the demands of school life at a level roughly appropriate to his or her age must have difficulties profound enough to warrant special educational placement.

The reason for the relative immunity of the educational system to the insights into children's development growing in other fields is interesting and not easy to explain. By the 1960s and '70s, however, those of us working in schools with children in difficulties were becoming increasingly aware of the formative importance of early experience. We thus greatly welcomed the Warnock Report for its implicit change of emphasis from category to process. Once process is centre stage the state of children on entry to school ceases to be regarded as largely the result of innate forces; instead awareness grows of what may lie behind unsatisfactory behaviour or achievements; this acknowledges the continuity of a child's life and thus the importance of early experience, and the differing attitudes and perceptions that this brings about.

Growth not pathology

Once the full import of this lack of good learning experiences is recognized, children in difficulties cease to be regarded as subnormal or disturbed but as children who have gone badly though the learning processes of early childhood and who therefore need extra support and appropriate experiences before they can learn in a normal school setting. In schools which set up nurture groups the emphasis, as Marjorie Boxall writes in the next chapter, is 'on growth not on pathology'. Teachers quickly begin to feel differently towards the children; they drop the load of guilt that will be familiar to any teacher who has been faced by a child who is failing. They begin to think differently about how to teach them, adapting their teaching strategies to meet the child's needs. With the experience of success they develop confidence that progress will be made. They are empowered to use their intuitive understanding together with their teaching skills, and job satisfaction changes significantly for the better.

Children in serious difficulties

Nurture groups have demonstrated that it is possible to give adequate help in mainstream school to children with difficulties serious enough to warrant urgent special placement. Such children often come from homes where there are serious social problems or parental inadequacy, perhaps violence between the parents, perhaps one parent has deserted the family, or where housing has been totally unsatisfactory; in short, from conditions where it has not been possible to meet the minimum developmental needs of the child. The children may present in school as withdrawn, sad, afraid to attempt work or to mix with other children; or they are aggressive to other children, unable to follow class routines, unresponsive to the efforts of their teacher to help them to overcome their difficulties. The teacher and the rest of the class suffer as well as the child with difficulties. Teachers not surprisingly often feel overwhelmed by the odds against them in working with children from such backgrounds. The nurture groups showed how normal teaching methods could be adapted to help such children effectively.

Nurture groups in Inner London

The groups spread quickly in the ILEA and were regularly monitored and evaluated. They were highly successful in keeping children in mainstream school; they were seen not only to help the children who were placed in them but to raise the morale of the whole staff by engaging them in positive discussions about the conditions underlying children's progress. By the late 1970s some 50 schools were taking part in the project and at a meeting at that time one head teacher after another reported great benefits to the children and great improvements in the confidence and morale of all the staff as their nurture group became established.[1] The number of teachers changing jobs, either to go to other schools or to leave teaching altogether, dropped significantly, as did the number of teachers taking sedatives to relieve work-related stress. The supportive 'whole-school approach', now so widely recommended, was achieved.

Integrated provision

The 1981 Education Act, which followed from the Warnock Report, made it official policy to keep children with special educational needs as far as possible in mainstream school. The Fish Report, *Educational Opportunities for All?* (ILEA, 1985) strongly supported this policy and drew attention to the work of nurture groups in achieving it:

> The concept of nurture work as normal pre-nursery learning for children who have not experienced many common domestic or material learning experiences, or whose stressful experiences have prevented them from profiting from them, is an important one. Much has been learned from this form of provision which could inform other special educational arrangements. Because it is based in schools, when the teachers work closely with others in the school it can help teachers of other classes gain insight and provide for children who might have special educational needs. (2.8.20)

As an approach with a clear rationale aimed at preventing many difficulties becoming special educational needs, it is to be endorsed. The intentions of nurture group provision accord with many of the Committee's principles, work being based in schools, closely linked with activities in the child's own class and providing a systematic approach to developmental difficulties. (2.8.23)

Meeting to respond to the committee of enquiry, a group of ILEA head teachers of primary schools with nurture groups pointed out how well nurture groups were already achieving integration or inclusion:[2]

- They are integrated provision.
- They are based on detailed observation and planning, are in the mainstream of good educational practice and contribute to it.
- They cater for children who need total environmental support, much more than peripatetic help can provide.
- Their conceptual basis makes sense and provides a purposeful framework for all staff.
- They are concerned with growth and so emphasize positive learning experiences, so that the potential of the child is more apparent.
- They provide a normal approach within the child's school environment and so provide continuity of educational experience.
- They exist within a mutually supportive school organization and ethos and contribute to it.
- They yield immediately available strategies and so generate optimism and cooperative nurturing attitudes throughout the school.
- To a major extent they avoid the need for sanctions, suspensions and Statements of Special Educational Need.
- For parents it is acceptable and positive provision. Some have refused other forms of help and have requested group placement. Many have daily contact with the group, value the teacher and welcome advice.

What happened to nurture groups?

The work of nurture groups spread almost by word of mouth. Marjorie Boxall lectured in London and elsewhere and the work of the groups aroused great interest. Visitors from many parts of the UK, from Sweden, Canada and New Zealand spent time in nurture groups or attended conferences, and many nurture groups were set up. They are recorded in Bristol, in Sheffield, in Newcastle, in Derby, in Bath and in Kent. But as there was no central organization, there is no systematic collection of information about them. It is highly likely that with the lead given by the Fish Report, nurture groups would have become part of official ILEA policy. But in London two things happened. Marjorie Boxall, who had been the central focus for the work, retired in late 1988 and in early 1989 ILEA was disbanded.

When the new London education authorities took over from ILEA, many of what became their schools had successful nurture groups and it is known that many of these continued. What is also known, although only anecdotally, is that although some educationists were very supportive, there was criticism from others who did not see the children's difficulties in terms of early developmental needs and felt, variously, that the groups were too permissive or too structured.

There were also some allegations of racism. On this point, it is true that there were many black children in the early groups. One reason for this is that the groups were in areas with large black populations. Also, black immigrants to London in the 1960s and '70s faced extremely harsh social conditions. There was the loss of extended family support; the loss of safe play space; poor housing conditions; the necessity for mothers to work long hours, often at the hardest and worst paid jobs; and a serious lack of good child-care facilities. Not surprisingly, many children came into school showing the effects of this stress. In a recent book *Black in White* (1995), Jean Harris-Hendriks, an English child psychiatrist, and John Figueroa, a Caribbean academic, discuss the matter:

> In the late 1960s a phrase, 'West Indian autism' had brief currency. It was racist, since it attributed to a particular culture a problem common to all children who are under-stimulated; that they are expressionless, unresponsive even when attempts are made to stimulate them, delayed in speech and motor skills and may end up stimulating themselves by repetitive behaviours such as rocking.
>
> In the early seventies many Inner London schools started 'nurture groups'. These were invaluable and deceptively simple arrangements whereby young children who for whatever reason, and irrespective of their nationality or skin colour, were unprepared to cope with pre-school and primary school, were lovingly and systematically taught the skills to care for themselves, the language to communicate with other children and enabled to play. The results were invaluable to the children, their teachers and their parents and it is sad to record that, because so many small black children joined these groups, the provision in the end was labelled as racist. This was the view of some educationists, including those of the same skin colour as the children, but not of the parents who valued what was being offered and could see how their children benefited. The children lost out, whatever their skin colour.

It is sad and ironic that anyone felt the groups to be in any way racist. Marjorie Boxall's admiration for the strengths and resourcefulness of Afro-Caribbean families in London had been reinforced by a visit to Jamaica in 1974, when she was a member of a group of educationists sent to try to understand better the difficulties that Jamaican children were facing in UK schools. Furthermore, it seemed to her that, generally speaking, children from Afro-Caribbean families made a faster response to the help offered in the nurture groups than children from the indigenous population. A likely explanation of this is that a major cause of stress for the black families was the result of their being new immigrants; whereas the difficulties in indigenous families would be more likely to be based on more specific and chronic weaknesses.

Nurture groups in Enfield

Happily, the experience and skills of the nurture groups were not lost. In the mid-1970s, Eva Holmes, an educational psychologist who had worked with Marjorie Boxall in Hackney, was working at the Tavistock Clinic in London. She helped to set up a special class attached to a day-nursery in Inner London whose aim was to prevent the need for special school placement for children who already by the age of three were disturbed in their behaviour or retarded in their development. Influenced by the rapid growth in understanding of the developmental processes of early childhood and aware of the success of the nurture groups, she introduced teaching based on similar principles into a nursery class for children who were in day or residential care.

The children could hardly have come from more disadvantaged backgrounds. 'Many had parents with a history of mental illness, drug abuse, alcoholism, attempted suicide, child abuse, violence and marital difficulties; in addition there are financial and housing problems.' The groups were small enough to allow adequate attention to each child, including individual discussions which could link events in the child's life over a period of time – for many, a new experience. As in the nurture groups, there was only a limited choice of an activity, with individual help to see it through to a satisfying conclusion.

The reliability and predictability of the adults were central. When the teacher was away ill, she sent the children postcards and telephoned them. The children then 'understood for the first time, it seemed, that a person could be absent but continue to exist and think about them'. In a reliable and regular setting, trust in adults grew and with it self-confidence. The child, often for the first time, could begin to feel that he or she could make predictions.

When I arrive, she will listen to what I say, my book will be in my box, there will be no interruptions and no unexpected visitors, I will be able to find my puzzle, if I need help I know I can ask; if someone else is painting, I know my turn will be next.

He begins to feel some control in this area of his life and will be able to take some initiative – try something new, go on trying, if it is difficult ask for help, perhaps eventually be able to put himself in the place of another child and help him to look ahead and reflect on yesterday. The teacher values him and he begins to value himself. (Holmes, 1980)

Impressed by the progress the children made, Eva Holmes set up a research project to measure the effects of this special intervention. The children in the special class formed the experimental group; the control group consisted of children who were also in day or residential care. Later, a group of children attending another day nursery, from apparently stable backgrounds, was added to the control group.

Both the children in the experimental and in the first control groups were assessed individually on admission to their nursery, at school entry and after a year in school. The measures used included a standard intelligence test and a scale of adjustment to school. There was no significant difference in measured intelligence between the experimental and the control group on admission to their nurseries; the average IQ for both groups being 84, i.e. somewhat below average. At age $4^{1}/_{2}$, the experimental group's IQ had gone up on average to 96.5, while the control group remained at 84. Looking at adjustment to school, the experimental group had scores at least as good as a normal group. As for their response to school, 'at 6 years most of them were still doing well in ordinary infant schools, whereas the majority of the control group had already been referred for or transferred to some form of special education' (Holmes, 1982).

Although the numbers in this study were small, outcomes in the experimental group were consistently and clearly better than those in the control group, even though the latter continued to receive the ordinary care and stimulation of a day nursery. Reading the two accounts of the project, the evidence is convincing that skilled, emotionally sensitive and precisely structured teaching intervention radically changed the educational prospects of severely disadvantaged children. This is exactly the message of Boxall's nurture groups and when Eva Holmes became principal educational psychologist of the London Borough of Enfield in 1981 she began with the support of the LEA to set up nurture groups. In 1996 these flourished in six of the authority's schools and much of the material for later chapters of this book is drawn from these groups.

The Code of Practice

The 1993 Education Act's Code of Practice was intended to identify and help children in difficulties in mainstream school before they reach the stage of needing special provision. The children who cause schools the greatest concern are those with emotional and behavioural difficulties. The Association of Workers for Children with Emotional and Behavioural Difficulties has been inundated with requests from schools to give the help needed by such children if the Code is to be implemented. When the ideas and methods of the nurture groups are discussed with any group of primary school teachers there is an immediate and positive response. Many teachers are already well aware of the connection between educational failure and the lack of adequate early experiences. When shown how good teaching practice and school organization can be adapted to teach such children successfully, there is a delighted recognition of an approach already almost understood. The question is then asked, 'Where can we find out about nurture groups?' This book is a first response.

NOTES

1. Personal communication from the late Norah L. Gibbs, head of the postgraduate training course in educational psychology at the Child Guidance Training Centre, London.
2. From Nurture Group archives held by Marjorie Boxall.

Chapter 2

The Nurture Group in the Primary School

Marjorie Boxall

The nature of the problem – the deprived child at home and in school

In Inner London in the 1960s, increasing numbers of children admitted to school were unable to meet the expectations and demands of an ordinary nursery or infant class. Their personal organization was poor and they showed learning and personality difficulties to varying degrees, and in some cases behaviour problems which led to disruption of the class. The more severe cases were usually referred to the Child Guidance Clinics, but psychotherapy was rarely felt to be relevant. The problems seemed linked with long-standing and continuing deprivation, and for this reason many of the children were referred on to special schools for educationally subnormal or for maladjusted children, as they were then termed, for these provided a modified situation offering greater personal support.

Many of these children lived under conditions of hardship and stress, in overburdened and fragmented families where relationships were eroded and strained, sometimes destructive and even violent. In some cases there was sudden and unexpected loss and change. The mother was under stress and this could affect the child from the beginning. In the early days she may have been too preoccupied or depressed to respond to her baby's mood and needs, and involve herself in his interest in the world. Even when this was a satisfying time for mother and child the sustaining interaction between them was in some cases abruptly impaired by sudden harsh weaning, often coinciding with a restriction on exploration and play, punitive management and sometimes neglect.

This was often the point when the child was handed over to babyminders, unskilled, and often as overburdened as the mother, with the additional fragmentation of experience this involved. (There was little control in the 1960s over standards in privately arranged child care, and much of it was of a poor quality.) In some families life was less damaging, and the problem seemed mainly to be the management of assertive and resistive behaviour. This was especially so where the parents had themselves been deprived children, for their emotional resources were slender and the stress of demanding and difficult children could be the last straw; they became over-controlling, punitive or erratic in their behaviour, and what they said and did might be more relevant to their own feelings and mood than to those of the child.

The crucial loss to the child is likely to be the continuing and constructive interaction through which he feels secure, gains a cohesive identity and internalizes concepts, skills and controls as he is helped to explore relationships and to control his own behaviour. Not surprisingly, children deprived in these ways are likely to grow up with a confused impression of themselves and the world, little sense of stability and sequence, a fragile identity and poor self-control. Where life is damaging and frustrating, aggression is frequently a major problem, though some children become inhibited, while others barely function.

School

School, whether infant or nursery, is based on the assumption that the children are essentially biddable, will be willing to entrust themselves to the teacher and will have some understanding of her expectations. It presupposes that they have an awareness of how the world about them functions, are sufficiently well organized to attend and follow through what is required without being constantly reminded, and that they already have some sense of time through the comfort and security of routines established at home. Furthermore, the children are now in a large group situation and must therefore be able to wait when this is necessary, to give and take with the others, and to have some tolerance for frustration. School thus continues a learning process which began years before in the home.

These assumptions are not necessarily true for severely deprived and disadvantaged children. They do not always accept the teacher as a trustworthy and reliable person, and do not attach themselves with confidence; they cannot engage with the situation and they do not learn. The problems may well worsen as the child grows older, for they are cumulative as the gap widens. Many teachers intuitively recognize that the children lack the foundations that are essential for further learning and try to help them at an earlier level. The strain of meeting such a wide range of social, emotional and intellectual needs is, however, sometimes too great for the teacher who becomes like the children, eroded and fragmented, and even sometimes resistive and hostile.

The rationale of the nurture group

The problems of such children are assumed to stem from the erosion of early care and support in families suffering severe social fragmentation and stress. Crucially, constructive forward-moving interaction with the child is lost. He does not therefore experience the reliable sequences of events that would develop in him an expectant attentiveness and through which he would gain an understanding of the world about him, and trust is weakened because the level of help and support he gets does not sufficiently or reliably meet his needs.

In the nurture group the teacher and helper attempt to relive with the child the missed nurturing experience of the early years. They take as their model the mother and her young child and the method is correspondingly intuitive: teacher and helper 'feel into' the early years and interact with the child as a mother would within a relationship of continuing care and support, in an environment that is carefully managed and protective.

The setting is a domestic one, and there is scope for unhurried experiences at a baby and toddler level. The nurture teacher and helper allow the child to be and help him to do; they keep him close emotionally and gradually let him go as he becomes increasingly able to manage on his own. The general guideline to which the teacher and helper return whenever in doubt is: 'this child is 3, 2, 1 year old, in some cases even younger. I will be for him and do for him as I would for my own child at that age'.

This guideline is reassuring; it yields insights into the needs of the children, and from it flows a wide range of stratagems. But an essential prerequisite for these adult-centred experiences is a school day that is planned and structured appropriately for this early developmental level and in which experiences are controlled and are basic and focused. Protected from the overwhelming stimulation and complexity of the ordinary class, the child is free within the constraints imposed by the nurture group to function at his 'true' developmental level. The teacher and helper respond accordingly and early level experiences and relationships follow. The first and essential consideration, therefore, when setting up a nurture group is structure. This is loosened as the child develops, but without the initial tight structure the process will fail.

Recreating the processes of adequate parenting in the nurture group

Satisfactory emotional, social and cognitive development in the earliest years is the product of adequate and attentive early nurturing care. It is a many-stranded, intermeshing, forward-moving, unitary learning process that centres on attachment and trust and has its foundations in the close identification of parent and child, and the interaction and participation in shared experiences that stem from this. It is the first stage of a developmental process through which the child builds up adequate concepts and skills, learns to interact and share with others and feel concern for them. Through this process he becomes increasingly self-supporting and self-directing and able to profit from the learning experiences offered at school.

But the child who has not experienced satisfactorily this early nurture-based stage of learning will not be able to engage with normal, age-appropriate school provision and will fail if the loss is not quickly made good. The task of the nurture group is to give the child the opportunity to go through these missed early experiences by creating a setting conducive to early developmental learning. Understanding the determinants of this process is of primary importance: the content then follows.

The determinants of early developmental learning

The constraints of early childhood

The nurturing context of early childhood is set by the child's physical status at birth, by his physical dependence and need for protection, by his motor and sensory development and the rhythm of his physical needs. These factors, and the intuitive involvement of his mother at the appropriate level, determine the things that interest him and to which he gives his attention, and lead to experiences that are restricted and highly focused at first. The constraints that determine these experiences are intrinsic to the early stages of childhood. They have to be deliberately built into the nurture group and in this way the situation is made appropriate for an earlier developmental level: simpler, more immediate, more protected. The child engages at this level, their attention is held, they experience pleasure and approval and basic experiences are consolidated. Rhythm and routines give security and a sense of order and they learn to anticipate events with confidence and interest.

In the home, there is emotional and physical attachment and proximity from the beginning. The waking day is short and slow moving, broken up by rests and simple, repetitive routines; management of the child's needs is consistent. Within this structure, the parents intuitively provide manageable learning experiences through appropriate play material and developmentally relevant interaction.

In the nurture group, close proximity in the home area of the classroom facilitates emotional and physical attachment. Early basic experiences are made available and are controlled by the teacher and helper, who direct the child's attention to features that are developmentally relevant. Everything is taken slowly and the day is broken up by slow-moving routines and interludes. There is a clear time structure; order and routine are emphasized, management of behaviour is consistent.

In these ways the growth-promoting patterns which the child missed in the early years in the home are established.

Attachment: earliest learning

In the earliest years the foundations of trust and security, positive mood and identity are built in through continuing support and shared basic satisfactions in the context of emotional attachment and physical proximity of the child and the adult. Feelings are communicated and shared, there is an understanding of subtle non-verbal signals and close identification and empathy, the one with the other. Developing with this is a shared experience, registered in language, of the basic attributes of objects, and simple cause and effect, leading to an understanding of objects and their relationships. These are the first and crucial stages of learning.

In both the home and the nurture group there is food, comfort, consistent care and support, and close physical contact seen in cradling, rocking, sensory exploration and communication by touch. Eye contact is central to the parent–child dyad and has to be purposefully established in the group. Mood and feelings are communicated through expression in face and in voice, with a spontaneous exaggeration of response. There is closeness, intimate interplay, shared feelings and satisfactions, with verbal accompaniment and the expression of mutual pleasure. Expectations are limited and infantile behaviour is accepted but the situation is kept safe and under adult control.

The first stages of learning are being consolidated.

Letting go and bringing back: developing autonomy

The child has already internalized the security that comes from attachment to a reliable, attentive, comforting parent and this security is reinforced through the continuing repetition of the simple routines of his daily life. These become a familiar and meaningful sequence of events and through these the child gains a sense that the world about him is stable, orderly and predictable. In the course of maturation and the appropriate opportunities provided he has acquired basic competencies. He has also experienced adequately consistent management of his behaviour, achieved and conveyed by explicit setting of boundaries.

From this secure base, the parents help the child to personal autonomy through a complex process of 'letting go' and 'bringing back'. He is 'let go' into experiences that the parents control and ensure are manageable and where support is provided when needed, and he is 'brought back' to the security of close contact with the parents when the situation is overwhelming and he can no longer cope. Because the parent is sensitively involved and intervenes when necessary, new experiences are manageable and the child is able to assimilate and consolidate them. He becomes personally better organized and learns to give and take and control his own behaviour; he explores with purpose and confidence, makes constructive relationships and realizes that he has some control over his environment.

In the home, the child does things with mother or with mother nearby. In the nurture group it is the teacher or helper who is with the child or nearby. In both there is frequent contact and reassurance, and expression of pleasure and approval, with the children in the group being collected together frequently, calmly, with eye contact re-established. In the home there is a spontaneously arising need for 'transitional objects' (to use Winnicott's term for the battered toy or piece of blanket from which so many young children are inseparable) to provide comfort, support and control. In the group the teacher or helper satisfy this need by making these available and encouraging their use.

Young children at home engage in simple experiment and repetitive play and of their own accord persist at this level and so, in the group, early play is introduced and if necessary is demonstrated; the experiment and repetition characteristic of this stage is given support and children are encouraged and helped to persist. In the home, children do not experience unnecessary frustration because their level of physical development and the mother's intervention determine the nature of their investigation and exploration. However, because children in the group are older their physical development is ahead of their experience and organization and they can therefore get into situations that are beyond their competence and overwhelm them.

The adult, therefore, selects activities for children's investigation and exploration; experiences are basic, controlled and directed; unmanageable situations are anticipated and avoided. And just as the mother responds with pleasure to each new achievement, the teacher or helper gives immediate praise for each small gain. The mother helps or intervenes when necessary and often plays with her child for mutual enjoyment; they share experiences and learn together and this is important in the nurture group too. In the home children are related to individually; the child, the object and the task are intuitively identified by name and the adults provide a running commentary. Similarly, early in the group, requests and instructions are always individual, never general; each child, object and task is deliberately named and there is continuing verbalization.

Normal early development is gradual, and in the course of physical maturation simple experiences come before complex ones and so, in the group, everything is provided in incremental stages with basic experiences coming first; situations are structured, essentials are highlighted and complex instructions are broken down. Sharing and choosing in the preschool years similarly come in manageable stages and there is little need to cooperate with other children. There is space to play and the mother anticipates problems. Correspondingly, in the group the need to share and choose is at first limited. There is always enough for everyone; sharing and choosing are built in manageable stages; grabbing is controlled; play space is respected. Cooperative work and play is not expected at this stage but it is encouraged, introduced and controlled and, as in the home, the teacher and helper anticipate problems.

The young child in the home needs and demands order and the mother meets her own and the child's need for order. In the group, therefore, as in the home, there is simple, consistent and unremitting basic training; the child is involved in orderly routines, tidying up, sorting out and putting away, with the adult giving help and reminders as they are needed. Expectations are made clear and constantly stressed; what is required is demonstrated. Approval and disapproval are immediate and evident; there is verbal commentary and reinforcement appropriate to an early level.

Children can now manage on their own for limited periods in a familiar environment. They are beginning to take responsibility for their own behaviour and will soon be able to take part without direct help in a bigger group. The foundations of their autonomy are becoming established.

Selection of children for the nurture group: pre-nursery needs

Selection of the children is made by the school. The criterion is the children's inability to engage themselves constructively in the day-to-day life of the class because of difficulties which seem crucially linked with impoverished experiences in the early years. These difficulties cover a wide range and include children who are unresponsive and never speak, those who are violently aggressive and disruptive and in the extreme case are markedly anti-social; others again who are unhappy, unventuring children, sometimes severely disturbed.

The problems are many and varied and we suppose, from the nature of the difficulties and the needs shown by the children, supported by case histories when we have these, that early nurture has been impaired in one or many of the ways outlined already. But although the ensuing problems vary with the nature and extent of the stress and with age, the children have in common a need for help at a pre-nursery level. Broadly based opportunities at an early stage are therefore made available in the nurture group; the children take from these the experiences they need, and the teacher and helper respond accordingly.

Organization within the school

Nurture groups have on average 12 children at any one time, but it is usual for many more children than this to go through the group in a year. A classroom preferably, or, failing this, a hut in the playground, is provided with comfortable domestic furnishings as well as work and play space. The relaxed setting is particularly important.

The nurture concept is implemented in different ways. Most schools have children in the group full-time, always with some interaction with the mainstream of the school from the beginning. Some have modified the basic pattern and admit some of the children part-time, while in others virtually all the children are part-time. One practice is to use the nurture facilities for new entrants felt to be 'at risk'. These variations reflect the nature and distribution of problems in the school as a whole and the range of competent functioning in the ordinary class. Whatever the approach, it is generally felt that some children need a full-time nurturing experience, while others actively benefit from greater contact with the ordinary class. The difference between full- and part-time nurture groups is thus largely one of emphasis.

The aim of the nurture teacher is to get the child back into an ordinary class. The child must therefore not feel, nor be felt by others to be, separate and different from the other children in the school. Indeed, he or she is not a special category of child; merely in one way or another at the extreme end of a continuum of disadvantage, often multiple, and in the ordinary class there are other children who are not very different. For these reasons the nurture group is fully part of the school, a resource with flexible boundaries for both teachers and children. This is fostered in different ways. In some schools the nurture children register with their class and are helped to feel part of that class, while in many schools extra children regularly go into the nurture room to play, often before school begins. In some schools the class teacher has 'breakfast' with the nurture group from time to time, or joins them for a birthday party. The nurture teacher or helper might go into the ordinary class to help the children settle in or, when a group runs only in the mornings, might work alongside the class teacher to give support to children in need.

Sympathetic rapport and good communication between the nurture teacher and class teacher is clearly important, each sharing an interest in the children's progress, and reinforcing what the other one does. Logically this implies a nurture orientation throughout the school, with all the teachers and ancillary staff in sympathy with the approach. The head teacher is the key person in fostering a good working partnership with the nurture group teacher, and the good relationships throughout the school as a whole on which the work depends.

In general the trend in schools with established nurture groups is towards nurture provision at the earliest possible age. Where the need is widespread, the more intensive work is done within the nurture group on a part- or full-time basis, but the other classes are modified accordingly and have an increasing and supportive involvement with the parents.

The activities and management of the nurture group

The brief account which follows is taken from the collated material from infant and junior groups where a high proportion of the children were impulse-dominated and had serious problems of aggression. It attempts to bring out the pre-school principles involved but the emphasis varies from one group of children to another, and in some schools is more explicit than in others. The detailed planning and structuring of the child's experience is not always apparent, as is the case in a well-functioning ordinary class where the organization of the teacher does not obtrude. Similarly, the baby behaviour of the children, so vivid in description, takes its place as a transient, though intense and necessary, developmental need. This need might suddenly change, and a child who has been wearing a pretend nappy one moment might be absorbed in a constructional game the next. To a visitor the most striking feature might well be the easy physical contact between adult and child, the warmth and intimacy of the family atmosphere, and the good-humoured acceptance, with control, of infantile and resistive behaviour.

General approach

The relaxed setting facilitates close physical proximity and eye contact, and the children become aware, often for the first time, of the adult's face, her expression, her gestures, the tone in her voice and what all these mean. Eye contact is of crucial importance and for most of the children can be established many times during the day when they are collected together in the 'home' area, for here they are able to settle and wait and attend.

In many different ways a close tie with the teacher and helper is established and maintained, and individual supports are built in because the children are too inexperienced to manage on their own. In the early days toys and work would be handed to the children individually, and instructions and requests would be specific to each child, spoken quietly in close physical proximity, with eye contact and touch where necessary. Teacher and helper settle the children down individually, giving simple reminders with much repetition. The complexity for the child of every task, however simple, is anticipated; it is broken down into stages and structured accordingly. Similarly there would be little or no choice at first because the children have no experience from which to exercise it; the biscuits offered at the breakfast table would be all the same and their toys would be chosen for them.

There is stress on tidying up and putting away in a particular place, because this basic training helps to build organization into the child; it gives him or her security, confident anticipation and prediction, and a sense of time. A slow pace is important, for the children need time to assimilate each stage; if taken on too quickly they become confused. Formal work, too, is structured, and for most of the children is at a very early level with much repetition. Children who are distractible in an ordinary class can give sustained attention to simple activities. The language of the teacher, as with the mother, instinctively matches the level of activity of the child and a running commentary, where appropriate, is a help in internalizing the experience and the expectations.

At this stage various braking techniques are built in, familiar and reassuring routines that control children's unchannelled energy, so that they attend and take in and feel satisfied. In ways such as these children's experiences and behaviour are monitored as by a mother. They are 'held' by the teacher. She controls the situation so that they are not bombarded, and gradually lets them go as they become better able to manage on their own. Stress in this situation is reduced and the problems are considerably relieved, particularly temper tantrums.

Children whose difficulties arise from inadequate and ill-organized experiences respond well in this secure setting. Others, however, have been managed erratically or punitively at home and present more serious behaviour problems. Control of their behaviour is an urgent priority and the strict and unremitting attention given to this in the groups is crucial. Desirable behaviour is constantly stressed and gets a positive response; undesirable behaviour like fighting is as far as possible ignored. The teacher's expectations are made absolutely clear and the only pressures in the group at this stage are those concerned with personal control. This is straightforward training: 'I see, I grab, I don't get.' Their teacher is always fair and gives a reason and the children quickly accept her requirements, adopt her standards for themselves, and support her in relation to the other children.

Food

Food is fundamental in the mother–child relationship and has special symbolic value. With few exceptions the children appear to experience the family-food occasions, or the giving of even a tiny sweet, as the expression of the teacher's and helper's attachment to them in a loving and caring relationship. It is part of their fabric of support, reassures them of their worth, and contributes to a sense of comfort and well-being. Some children, particularly the timid tearful ones, form this attachment from the beginning. Others do not, and food becomes part of a satisfying relationship only later when they acknowledge the teacher and attach themselves with trust. For these children, among whom are the particularly aggressive ones, food is not initially the expression of a relationship. Food is something they want; it may be at first the only thing to which they attend, and in attending to the food they attend to the teacher.

This may be the first time that eye contact is established, the first time they wait, and in waiting see themselves in relation to the teacher. At this stage food for these children, who may be virtually unmanageable, provides a powerful 'holding' situation affording maximum control. It is particularly important in the early days. In this situation, as in all others, the primitive behaviour which immediately becomes apparent in many of the children is not aggression but greed; if this is not anticipated, the children will grab at anything, and push and fight. This greed is controlled, as it is with toys and other experiences, by exposing the children to the situation in tolerable stages and not giving a surfeit; and praise is lavish, for the children are greedy also to be the best and get the most praise.

The timid inhibited children are reassured by the firm control, and the teacher–child equilibrium they see established helps them to be more assertive. In the more open situation of the ordinary class they hold back and get left out, and anything they have they keep to themselves. In the nurture group as they become less fearful they begin to eat and gradually they, too, learn to share. For all the children, 'family' food occasions provide an important opportunity to build in vital learning experiences: holding back, waiting, sharing, choosing, taking turns, giving up for others, anticipating their needs, and tolerating frustration. As one of the helpers put it, 'We have a tremendous palaver for a tiny piece of toast'. Food may be 'breakfast', perhaps no more than half a slice of toast and a choice of jam, or biscuits with their milk. Food for all the children becomes less important as time goes on; they take their security for granted and are free within themselves to become interested in other things.

Infantile needs and interests

All the children, whatever their difficulties, have available to them early infantile experiences. In both infant and junior groups a general need, in some cases intense, is for close physical contact with the teacher and helper. In some this seems primarily a need for reassurance and affection. In others there seems to be a need for attachment at the baby stage, and repeatedly a teacher or a helper describes the baby-like curl of the feet and the aimless baby-like movements. They lie on her lap and are cradled and rocked, stroke her hair and ruffle it; they play with her hands and her feet and her jewellery, and love to comb her hair. Some slip into baby sounds and crawl on the floor. They babble and jabber and want to be picked up, or they move in an uncoordinated way, fingers in their mouths. They pick things up and give them to their teacher, or bang them noisily on the table.

An interest in their bodies and its functions is shown by many of the children. For some of them this is absorbing and all-consuming and they describe their experiences in uninhibited detail. They readily identify with each other at this level and live each other's anecdotes with avid pleasure. With the older children this is more than an interested monologue; it is the stuff of their conversation. They have uninhibited sexual interests too; for most of the children these interests are childish and ephemeral and lively involvement one week has disappeared without trace by the next. In a few cases these interests seem likely to be reality-based and inappropriate sexual experiences may have been a major factor in the child's anxiety and disturbed behaviour.

Play

These early developmental stages link with the initial lack of interest shown by the children in small dolls and cuddly toys. They seem to move on to doll play, and caring for the dolls, only after their own need for affection has been met; in the early days it is they who wear the nappy and suck from the bottle, and play babies together and comb each other's hair and feed each other. But big stuffed dolls and animals are important to them at an early stage and are the object of fierce love and hate. Later they become members of the peer group, and a monkey in a junior school sits at the table, pencil in hand, wearing an anorak and doing his sums, while in another junior school a bear is given a book to read.

Many of the children have a special need to mess with paints, clay, water and sand and enjoy this at a sensuous level. Even junior children spend hours with the sand; they enjoy scooping it, and like to feel it and let it run through their fingers. They enjoy the water trough, too, blowing bubbles and experimenting for long periods of time. Many of them spend days in repetitive play, perhaps doing a simple jigsaw over and over again, or crashing the cars, or pushing and pulling heavy toys in the playground. For many children play is at first solitary, but they get used to playing alongside each other, and then gradually parallel and then cooperative play develops, becoming more elaborate as they act out their feelings and take on roles.

Occasionally the solitary and repetitive play seems a defence, a retreat from the world when it is all too much.

Whatever the level and nature of their play, the teacher and helper are available to share the experience, guide, put in ideas, or participate in the role demanded by the child and so contribute to the development of the play. At other times it may be more important for the children to play quietly at their feet as they talk.

Behaviour management: learning self-control

Most of the children in the nurture groups have serious behaviour problems; others, who at first barely function or are baby-like in their behaviour, go through a phase of fights and tantrums. Many of these outbursts have the quality of infantile fury and, as with a very young child, the incidents which provoke them are trivial, but they can be difficult to manage because the children are big and strong. The orderliness and organization of the day help to reduce the problems; they give shape to the children's behaviour and the manageable experiences provided engage their attention and direct their energy. This makes it easy after an upset to re-engage the child in a known and comfortable routine.

It is usually possible to avoid an escalation of trouble by intervening at the first sign of niggly interference; and if the group gets 'high' the children can generally be calmed by drawing them into the 'home' area and waiting until everyone is quiet and still. Many fights and tantrums can be averted because the children are dominated by immediate perceptions and it is easy, therefore, to attract their attention to something else. All these are stratagems that a mother would instinctively use with her very young child. Talking about the situations that provoke trouble, and the angry feelings the children have, is important. They are taught not to hit out when they have these feelings, but to keep them inside and show their annoyance in a more grown-up way; and they talk about other people's feelings and the sort of things that hurt.

Verbalizing in this way slows the children down; they are able to reflect on what they would otherwise do impulsively and in this way begin to internalize the teacher's expectations and controls. Games centring on facial expression and feelings also help, as does looking at themselves in a mirror because it makes them more aware of feelings that they have not recognized and helps to develop self-control.

In the early days of a difficult group a high-risk period is first thing in the morning, especially on Mondays, and 'breakfast', usually provided at about 10 o'clock, has a markedly stabilizing effect. If a fight does break out the children move away from the disturbance and carry on with their activities as they have been trained to do, for they are then less likely to suck in the anxiety and become inflamed by the aggression. The fight itself is, as far as possible, ignored. A child in a temper tantrum would be held until it was all over, or left to pummel the cushions; the teacher would talk about what had happened and when it was all over would explain about the sort of behaviour she likes, and would then give reassurance and support. Difficult groups seem to reach a crescendo of bad behaviour, fights and tantrums and then calm down and consolidate.

Becoming independent

The children in the groups are closely identified with the teacher and helper and this attachment is seen in the use of their belongings as 'transitional objects'. These provide a tangible link with the teacher and helper and seem to act as a symbol both of the child's attachment to the adult and of the adult's support and control. The children wear her jewellery, her poncho, and the more immature children particularly love to wear her scarf. Sometimes the adult leaves them with something to help them manage their feelings when she is not there. This might be a ribbon, tied on the child's wrist when they go on an outing, or the comment when she leaves him alone, 'Keep my seat warm, I won't be long.'

Sometimes the children give a clear indication of their need for the adult's comfort, support and control to be expressed in a tangible form. Thus a girl, running from the play centre when she saw her teacher leaving at the end of the day, asked for a kiss. Her teacher kissed her lightly because she had just put on her lipstick and didn't want to leave this on the child's face. 'No, kiss me properly;' said the child, 'I want your lipstick'.

Some of the children, typically the more aggressive ones, are excessively dependent on their teacher and in these cases separation might be initiated by the teacher. A nine-year-old boy would lie for long periods on his teacher's lap and followed her everywhere. She brought in a large 'gonk' which she cuddled on her knee during story time and the child cuddled up by her side. After a few days, if his teacher did not have the 'gonk' he would go looking for it and would sit with it and plait its hair and tie its arms round his wrist. It became important to him, satisfied his need for his teacher, and he did not go on her lap again.

These early needs and infantile protests are only a stage in the children's development, and as they become less dependent they move out into wider and more complex experiences. Choice is extended, frustrations are built-in in ways which are tolerable, and satisfactions are delayed. Group activities in the form of games with enjoyable rules and rituals are introduced. The content of the games centres on basic sensory and cognitive skills, personal identity and social awareness. The rules and rituals that are built into these games are an acceptable discipline when in the context of 'fun' and the sequence of satisfying events leading to the anticipated goal helps the children to delay gratification. Basic cognitive skills are also more readily built up in the non-threatening ambience of the games and these achievements contribute to the development of self-confidence and a feeling of personal worth.

Visits out are planned, but the children are always carefully prepared, are told what to expect and how to behave, and may practise in school beforehand. A favourite visit, when this is feasible, is to the helper's or teacher's home for a drink and cake and chat. Their interest in the teacher and helper is insatiable; they love hearing about their children and ask for the same anecdotes over and over again. Talking, too, is very important, when baking with the helper or sitting round the ironing board while she irons, or as a 'family' occasion over their drinks.

The children play a great deal in the group but need input from the teacher and helper in the form of suitable material and ideas, and comments that take the play forward. The teacher and helper also set up play projects which they exploit at every level. Games, too, carry learning experiences and are devised to meet needs of all kinds. 'Mother's lap', 'mother's knee' and 'mother's day' activities provide opportunities for the introduction of basic language, mathematics and science, and lend themselves quite naturally to explicit educational input from the teacher. All the children also attempt some kind of directed formal work, and although in some cases this is at a very early level, it is always linked with, or relevant to, the work of the ordinary class. This formal (now National Curriculum-oriented) work may quickly take up a substantial part of the day.

Adult relationships as a model

The relationship between the teacher and helper is of great importance, for this is often the only opportunity the children have of seeing constructive interaction between adults. For this reason the teacher and helper talk together, sharing views, demonstrate concern for each other, acknowledge courtesies, and have fun and laugh. The head teacher is also important, representing the wider world of school, and being seen to support and value the teacher and helper. It is usual and helpful for a man to be involved if only peripherally, perhaps the caretaker, or the husband of the helper or teacher. He is seen to support and value the helper or teacher; he might romp with the children or tell them a story, or join them for a game in the park.

Parental involvement

Parental involvement is encouraged but varies widely. Some parents are never seen, others are known only through home visits, others again call in at school from time to time, while others take part in the school day and may become very dependent on the relationship. The policy adopted varies from school to school, some using opportunities as they arise, while others have parents' evenings from time to time and make considerable efforts to encourage the parents to attend. Parents' evenings are informal social occasions affording an opportunity for teachers and parents to share views and air differences on such important themes as play, discipline and happiness in relation to learning. The parents, many of whom have previously been difficult to reach, feel valued for themselves, not just because they are parents of the children, and in some cases their response is overwhelming.

On these occasions it is useful to provide a variety of quickly accomplished tasks that have a pleasing outcome. This gives the parents some understanding of what is being done in school. It is also a relaxing and enjoyable experience which they share with the others, and this may be particularly important for parents who are socially isolated or new to this country. A few of the parents need as much help and support as their children, not only in understanding how to organize their materials, but in coping with frustration when things go wrong. Where possible, everyone in the family is invited to these evenings, and it is usual then for the children to prepare the food and hand it round. The importance for the children is that home and school visibly become one, for they see parent and teacher talking together on equal and friendly terms. With few exceptions the parents are content with the shared nurturing between home and school, and many have remarked with relief and pleasure on the children's improved behaviour at home and greater progress in school.

Measuring progress

We know that the children are making progress when they get satisfaction from pleasing the teacher and helper and from meeting their expectations. Clear standards of behaviour have been set and they now identify with these and show unease when they transgress the limits. Some of the children, however, are so ridden with fear that they dare not assert themselves or take what is legitimately theirs, and the first stage in their progress might be deliberately provocative and defiant behaviour, a phase of naughtiness through which they test out their new-found selves before they, too, begin to function constructively in the group. Others, again, are so disorganized and lacking in confidence that they are over-concerned to please and the first stage in their progress would be a lessening of this concern to please.

Consolidated progress is shown when the children begin to be concerned for and take pleasure in each other. They relate more constructively, share spontaneously, and can accept disappointments and tolerate frustration. They develop a sense of humour and can laugh at themselves. Their concentration and attention span improve and they become more friendly, more confident, and much, much happier. It is of interest that the children seem to experience the steps they take towards social maturity as lessons. They seem aware that the teacher is providing a learning experience and get a sense of satisfaction and achievement when they succeed. This is perhaps best expressed in the words of a particularly aggressive six-year-old girl, who remarked to the helper one day: 'Miss, it's a nice feeling, being good.' Not surprisingly, with this developing maturity comes a marked improvement in their academic work.

Getting back into the ordinary class

This more mature behaviour is built in through a close interaction with the teacher and helper; it becomes part of the child and is not imposed from without. The children become better able to participate in the group without direct help and as soon as they seem ready to manage are tried out in the ordinary class for short, carefully planned periods. This may be before they are quite ready, because there comes a critical point when greater progress is made in the ordinary class even though there may be difficulties at first. Boredom is a good indication that they are ready to move on. The situation, however, has to be carefully watched by everyone because the children's experience is still shaky and inadequate, their personal control is flimsy, and anxiety and panic may quickly surface.

Although some children settle in their ordinary classes with very little direct support, and in some cases may take the initiative to go, others need more help if they are not to be put into a situation where they will fail. The teacher or helper would assist children in preparing their things and might go with them to their class to settle them in. If another child is being 'weaned' at the same time, the two children might well go off together. A less secure child might take something from the teacher, perhaps a special pencil or her bracelet, as a comfort and support. The receiving teacher makes them welcome, and when they return to the nurture group at the end of the day, perhaps for 'tea' or a story, they talk about what they have done and might show their work. All these supports help them over the difficult early stages.

The Boxall Profile

Record-keeping is an important feature of nurture-work and central to this is the Boxall Profile, until 1998 known as the Diagnostic Developmental Profile (Bennathan and Boxall 1998). This was developed over several years in partnership with teachers, their co-workers and head teachers in ILEA schools which had nurture groups; it involved extensive discussion and frequent reappraisal.

For the first two years of the nurture groups, records of the children had taken an anecdotal form but teachers soon began to express a need for a better way of assessing children referred to the nurture groups. They wanted something which would quantify their impressions, that would alert the class teacher to features to look for and would provide a means of evaluating progress. The behaviours recorded by the teachers were in some cases the characteristics shown by normal young pre-nursery children, and were assumed to persist in older children because early developmental needs had not been met; in other cases the maladaptive behaviours seemed to be an attempt by a poorly organized and ill-supported child to meet the demands of everyday life in school, sometimes at the level of survival.

Work on the profile began in 1972. The behavioural characteristics of children in the nurture groups that were reminiscent of behaviour seen in normally developing children in the pre-nursery years were cast in the form of descriptive items. These were derived from teachers' and helpers' observations, either verbal contributions at meetings, in discussion, or recorded in their notes, or from impressions picked up on visits to the groups. They were discussed at nurture group meetings in terms of developmental expectations of pre-nursery children and were arranged in what was felt to be a developmental order. Teachers, helpers and head teachers all had a part in this. A contribution of one of the helpers stands out vividly. A toddler-like item was under discussion: 'engages in random investigation about the room (picks things up, shakes them, etc. but does not use them)'. 'Is into everything', the helper immediately said and this description remained part of the profile.

All the items discussed at this stage were normal features when seen in the young pre-nursery child but not all were normal in the school setting, where they could be disastrous. It seemed helpful, therefore, to pull out from this continuum features that remained positive as the child grew older, e.g. 'makes eye contact', and to add descriptions of adaptive, organized and constructive behaviour at a more autonomous level, features seen in a competently functioning school-age child, e.g. 'abides by the rules of an organized group game in the playground or school hall (interacts and cooperates and continues to take part for the duration of the game)'. These items formed section I of the profile. All the other items were either normal characteristics of the pre-nursery child that were maladaptive in the school setting, or they reflected more complex deviance. These items formed section II of the profile.

A viable profile emerged from these early discussions and was in use for a number of years. In 1978, the Research and Statistics Branch of ILEA, with funding support from the DES, undertook a statistical analysis of the data. In preparation for this, more intensive work was done on the items of the profile, involving teachers in schools unfamiliar with nurture work.

Two sections

Section I of the profile is named 'Developmental Strands'. It provides a description of the personal and social development of the school-age child from three to eight years, and gives helpful information about the class as a whole. The characteristics noted are those of the developing child that reflect or contribute to a constructive learning process, and they can be scored by the teacher from knowledge of each child in the course of ordinary school life. The statistical analysis indicated that these 34 descriptive items fell into two broad clusters, described as 'Organization of experience' (for example, 'makes appropriate and purposeful use of the/ materials/equipment/toys provided by the teacher without the need for continuing direct support') and as 'Internalization of controls' (for example, 'Looks up and makes eye contact when the teacher is nearby and addresses him by name, i.e. heeds the teacher').

Section II is named the 'Diagnostic Profile'. The statistical analysis of the 34 non-adaptive items drew them into three clusters, namely:

1 Self-limiting features, e.g. 'avoids, rejects or becomes upset when faced with a new and unfamiliar task, or a difficult or competitive situation'.

2. Undeveloped behaviour, e.g. 'restless or erratic; behaviour is without purposeful sequence, continuity or direction'.

3. Unsupported development, e.g. 'lacks trust in the adults' intentions and is wary of what they might do; avoids contact or readily shows fear'.

Section II shows areas of deviant behaviour that inhibit or interfere with the learning process, and in conjunction with Section I gives clear pointers to those children who would be well placed in the nurture group, those who need other skilled intervention and those who can be helped by appropriate support in the ordinary class.

Conclusion

The work done in the nurture groups is based on the attachment of the child to the teacher and helper at an early level of dependency. Through interaction at this level an expectation of ongoing support is established: the child trusts and teacher and helper build on this trust; the children accept the demands made of them because they are safe in their keeping. The approach is essentially an educational one for it is forward-looking and is concerned with every aspect of early learning. The focus is thus not on problems, but on growth and the conditions which facilitate growth. Clearly, the younger the child, the better the support provided by the whole school and the greater the involvement of the parents, the more likely is this growth to be initiated and maintained.

Those who have been closely concerned with this project have no doubt at all that growth and well-being can be fostered in children whose life situation is difficult and in many cases appalling beyond belief. The underlying hypothesis is a very simple one and can be implemented intuitively without the need for a lengthy theoretical training. The anxiety of the teacher and the helper is thereby reduced and they are enabled to draw maximally on their own resources; they are not inhibited by the feeling that somewhere there are experts who know better. They are self-reliant and secure in their own autonomy, have a clear sense of direction and a rough idea of the possibility of success with the different kinds of problems.

The work is thus approached with confidence and, because they give themselves unreservedly to the children, they draw on energies that were previously untapped. Teacher and helper have a greater sense of identity in their role, feel they are using themselves fully and, like all parents, they grow with the children. All work hard, but the stress is constructive, not frustrating; they give a great deal but are amply rewarded by the affection of the children and the joy of their progress. The relief to the other teachers is considerable; they become willing and interested partners in the children's development and cooperate in the process of reintegrating them into the ordinary class. The nurture group is also a help to the children who remain in the ordinary class, for the teacher has more time for them and their lessons are not disrupted by inappropriate behaviour.

For a group to function well and to be an integral part of the school it is essential that the principles underpinning nurture work are accepted and its complex and demanding nature is understood by all the staff members and others concerned with the school. The children in the nurture group are then valued members of the school, and the teacher and helper are also held in high regard. When this happens, the ethos of the school changes; optimism is generated, there is mutual understanding and support and concerted, constructive effort which benefits the whole school.

Chapter 3

Nurture Groups in the 1990s

Marion Bennathan

Nurture groups are known to exist in several parts of the UK across the continuum of special educational needs provision. Many residential schools for children with serious emotional and behavioural difficulties share the nurture groups' principles of making good the child's developmental loss and some have formal nurture groups. The ethos and methods have been found to work in all these settings. However, the groups most obviously fit the purposes of the 1993 Education Act when they are integrated provision, that is, when they encourage the early identification of difficulties at the first stages of the Code of Practice, contribute to keeping children in mainstream school and to a positive whole-school approach. Some LEAs such as Enfield have groups which are an integral part of a school's provision, available in the main only to children already in the school. In other LEAs, such as Newcastle-on-Tyne, they had an area function. Both these arrangements will be now be discussed.

The organization of nurture groups in Enfield

The London Borough of Enfield had, in 1996, six nurture groups in infant schools or departments, run with regular and agreed support from the authority's advisory staff and educational psychology service. Reporting on the groups' progress is part of the authority's regular overall audit of special educational needs. Monitoring of each child's progress is an essential part of the work of the groups and in addition there have been two in-depth studies, at M.Sc. level, of the work of the groups by educational psychologists in training at the Tavistock Institute in London.

The groups have fitted into the many changes in education following the 1988 and 1993 Education Acts, specifically to the requirements of the National Curriculum, and to changes in local authority funding. In Enfield, the schools with nurture groups receive fully delegated funding to cover the cost of the teacher and the assistant. With the Code of Practice now in place, the groups are regarded by their schools sometimes as Stage 2 provision but mainly as Stage 3, that is, in-school provision which does not require the child to have a statement of special educational need: this in itself is a considerable saving, since 'statementing' is a costly process. Much of what follows draws heavily on the authority's documentation about nurture groups, on discussions with and material prepared by their teachers and general assistants, and discussions with the authority's adviser and educational psychologists most closely concerned with the groups.

Which schools need a nurture group?

The size of school is important; one with at least two forms at each year level is considered desirable. Social conditions in the catchment area are relevant, such as the school having a larger proportion of its children entitled to free meals than other schools in the area; in Enfield, 30 per cent is regarded as a significantly large number. Other indicators would be that an audit of special educational needs shows a large number of children with emotional and behavioural difficulties; that there are significant levels of under-achievement at Key Stage 1; that there is a high proportion of children considered by the local Social Services Department to be at risk of abuse or neglect; that nursery or other pre-school provision is either lacking or not sufficient to meet specific nurturing needs.

A whole-school resource

It is a central principle in Enfield that there must be a commitment to the project from all the staff and from the governors of the school. The head teacher's wholehearted support is essential. He or she takes overall responsibility for the group and is committed to meeting regularly with group staff and to taking part, together with the school's educational psychologist, in decisions about admissions to the group and reintegration into the normal class. The nurture group forms part of the school's special educational needs provision, and is referred to in the school's formal policy on special educational needs which is required by the authority's procedures. The group's teacher and assistant cannot be used to cover for absent staff in the rest of the school.

The staff of all the authority's nurture groups meet regularly for two hours in-service training each month, a meeting that is given high priority because it is considered essential for keeping up standards. The coordinating role in this is taken by the deputy head teacher of one of the schools, herself a former nurture group teacher, who is also the special educational needs coordinator for her school and therefore in a support role to the school's group. The group's teacher is responsible for the day-to-day running of the class. This includes organizing and planning teaching, keeping records of each child's progress and programmes of work, encouraging parental involvement in the child's development, keeping close contact with the child's class teacher and other staff, and taking part in in-service training. The nurture group assistant is employed in the group full-time, working under the guidance of the group teacher. His or her role is to join with the teacher in whatever tasks are necessary in the group, to contribute to record-keeping and to take part in the regular in-service meetings.

The nurture group is an integral part of the school

In Enfield, the nurture group is an integral part of the school and so follows the school's policies, for example on language, literacy and numeracy, on child protection, and on equal opportunities. It is well understood by all nurture group staff that their purpose is to enable children who are under-achieving, due to a lack of pre-school experience and to social deprivation, to gain the experience necessary to overcome their difficulties and where possible be successfully reintegrated fully into their mainstream class. Each group's role is to serve the children, parents and teachers in their school.

All the children continue to belong to a mainstream class and while there are treated as full class members, having their own tidy-tray, workbooks, coat hook and work place in the same way as other class members, and with the class teacher encouraging the child to feel part of the class. While the group children are away from the classroom the rest of the class can function free from the stress which their presence often brings. Nurture group children are also encouraged to take part in all school activities including playtimes, physical education, assemblies and outside visits, although sometimes they will need to stay in the group with teacher and assistant because they cannot for the moment cope with the ordinary demands of a larger group of children.

Organizing a nurture group

The groups have a maximum of ten children in them and the composition of the group has to be considered carefully, for example, the ratio of boys to girls, and even more important, the mixture of aggressive, disruptive and withdrawn, introverted, fearful children. This is to create a balanced group which functions constructively. The aim is always to provide a secure and stable learning environment where children can learn through experiencing pre-school nurture from two caring and reliable adults. The authority's guidelines quote Marjorie Boxall: 'This child is behaving as a 3, 2, 1 year old, in some cases even younger. I will be for him/her and do for him/her as I would for a child of my own at that age.' As the children develop trusting relationships with the adults their self-confidence grows and they begin to use their curiosity to learn at levels more appropriate to their age; gradually they learn how to control their behaviour.

The children have already made it obvious that they are unable to cope in a normal classroom, so the nurture group environment is one of home-like warmth, comfort and security with a kitchen area, a dining area and a comfortable sitting area with sofas. Ideally there should be space for sand and water play. A full-length mirror has been found to be an essential aid to formal and informal work on self-awareness, which is part of developing self-control. There is also an area set out for formal work.

Nurture group routines

One of the Enfield groups prepared some guidelines for new groups setting out, intended as a helpful starting point rather than a rigid prescription. They note that it is important to have an outline of the day that is absolutely clear both to staff and children because the children, by their very nature, bring their own element of unpredictability. They recommend that the structure, as well as clear individual education plans, should be conveyed with empathy and a sense of humour.

While each school may organize its group somewhat differently, there are agreed procedures which are discussed and reviewed at LEA level. On a typical day, therefore, children will be registered with their base class from where the nurture group staff will collect them. There will be a group session in the sitting area, with news followed by discussions about activities and carefully controlled decision-making about what to choose. There will then be art or craft activities. Then will come the time for a drink and something to eat, often called 'breakfast'. This is a time for children to learn social skills, cooperating in laying the table, handing the food round, learning to take turns, sometimes having to be last. Then there is clearing away, washing up, all with an emphasis on considering the needs of others. Next will come formal work, often for short periods at first, gradually extending as concentration improves so that confidence builds up as success is achieved. The session may end with a television or radio programme, music time, sewing, computers, individual reading, or a group story time.

Although there is variation from day to day, there is always an explicit emphasis on what is coming next, warnings of change, and frequent rehearsals of adult expectations. A much greater degree of control than is possible or necessary in the mainstream class is given, affectionately and with much recognition of improvement. As children gradually internalize the order and routine they begin to manage themselves much more successfully. They become calm and confident that what has been promised will be given.

After the first afternoon session, the nurture group children will return to their mainstream class for the end of afternoon activities. This gives the group teacher and assistant time to discuss their observations of each child during the day and to write up their daily records which detail what has happened to each child on that day and note down as much positive information as possible as well as any behaviour or learning patterns that emerge. These would then be used to modify the child's individual education programme. A typical day would be like this:

8.30	Both staff arrive, discuss the plan for the day, any extra events that may be happening within school which might affect the group. Prepare the room.
9.05	Jointly go to collect the children from their base classes.
9.15	Return with the whole group to the nurture group room for group time, with children sitting on the carpet. During this time, the group works as a whole on such topics as the state of the weather, the days of the week, numbers, reading or word recognition or number work.
9.30	The children will have been sitting on the carpet for 15 minutes and they need to move around a little. They go and work individually on drawing and writing in their diary. Then there is free choice of an activity from a selection of equipment already set out. This gives individual children an opportunity to have some time with an adult to share an activity or a concern. One or two children help to prepare 'breakfast'.
9.55	The children wash their hands ready for 'breakfast'.
10.05	'Breakfast', which is eaten sitting around the table together, can be toast and a selection of spreads, a cake to celebrate a birthday, or food that the children have made, perhaps linked to a television programme. There is a choice of drinks: milk, a hot drink, or fruit squashes. Sharing food assists in creating emotional attachment and cementing a loving and caring relationship. It is an ideal opportunity to sit down all together, a new experience for some of the children, and to pay attention to and to talk to each other. Other social skills are practised, such as learning to share. Children may be given tasks

to increase their independence, as, for example, going without an adult to the nursery to fetch the milk, a popular and status-giving task. After breakfast is finished the children help to clear up.

10.25 The whole group listens to a radio programme such as 'Wriggly Park', a popular programme for young children, to encourage listening and memory skills. They sing and join in the actions, which helps their coordination and encourages them to enjoy each other's company.

10.40 Playtime: the group children join the rest of the school in the playground. If they are having real difficulties there they may be allowed to stay in the group room with a friend. Sometimes nurture group staff go into the playground to help them join in with other children. Sharing playtime when they can manage it gives them a chance to build up friendships with their classmates, an important ingredient in keeping them a member of their class and preparing them eventually to return there. A successful playtime also builds up a positive profile for the child among classmates and other staff.

11.00 The children return to the group or, if they are very young or in need of support, they are collected from the playground. The children gather together sitting on the carpet. It is in this session that more formal work takes place. There may be some phonic work with 'Letterland' as the basis, or they may share a story. Starting this session as a group has been found to be valuable. It gives the children the opportunity to discuss playtime experiences and for the adults to sort out any violations of rules that have gone unnoticed in the playground. Reprisals are thereby defused.

The children are also given another experience of functioning as part of a small group, learning to be attentive to others and to wait their turn, vital skills for successful learning in the large class where so often the group children have been disruptive. After the group activity all the children move to their place at the tables to do formal work at their own level. It has been found essential for all the children to start this at the same time, because many of them had difficulty in functioning well if other children were 'playing' so that much energy went into feeling resentful.

As the children complete the task as planned with the adult, they choose an alternative activity.

11.55   The children are returned to their base class for lunch. How this is done depends on each child's level of confidence or self-control; they may escort a younger member of the group back to their class teacher, or an adult may take them back to their own class, or they may join their class as it passes the group room to go to the toilets. This last tactic is better for children who are still not able to manage in the bigger group. It was found that joining their own class as the children there were in the process of bringing their session to a close could create problems, whereas feeding the child into their class line on the move or directly into the teacher's hand gave the child who needed it the necessary sense of structure and of belonging.

12.00 Dinnertime   Together with the other staff members, the dinner supervisors are involved in what the group is aiming to achieve with its charges, so that they can behave supportively. Since many of the group children are still at the egocentric stage of needing to be assured of their own apparatus and play space, it was thought that providing small skills apparatus, such as soft balls, skittles and floor dominoes for use in the playground would help dinnertime behaviour. It is found that the greater the structure the easier it is for many of the children to manage dinnertime well, which raises their self-esteem and reputation among their classmates and the school staff. (Interestingly, the greater structure set up for the nurture group children was found helpful to the rest of the children in the school as well.)

13.30   After dinner the children are once again collected from their classrooms. Sometimes their class teacher invites them to stay and participate in a special class activity. Alternatively, and by previous arrangement, the children frequently bring a friend to the group from their class. This assists the group child's sense of belonging to the larger group and also fosters class friendships which are vital if the transition-back process is to be successful. Bringing a friend to the group allows the group child to be seen more positively by other children. The friend may also provide a useful role model for the group children and, importantly, keeps the staff in touch with age-appropriate behaviour.

13.40   There is a quiet story time to settle the children down.

13.55 The next hour is usually devoted to craft sessions. Group children are unable to sustain art work for any length of time so lengthy projects such as friezes are rarely attempted; instead, short activities involving a variety of artistic experiences are provided. After this, the children choose from a variety of play activities which may include games which encourage language and literacy skills. Once a week there is cooking. The play house and playing hairdressers are very popular and the staff get involved in these. Many of the children have had little positive and consistent interaction with adults, so that actually playing constructively with one is a novel and important experience for them. Sometimes, sharing a game in the corner needs to take precedence over work on reading. Staff sometimes have to remind themselves to respond as a mother with the child's needs and stage of development in mind, rather than as a teacher always attempting to achieve age-related norms.

At the end of this hour a point is made of reminding the group before they leave of any changes there might be on the following day. A predictable routine is especially important to these children who often lead very erratic lives; by always preparing them for changes they are helped to build up and internalize a sense of order.

Tidying up time can be a nightmare. It is an ideal opportunity to get up to mischief, deliberately breaking someone's model under the guise of tidying it away. It is found that it works best for a couple of children to take turns to tidy up under supervision while the rest of the group look at a book while sitting on the carpet.

14.55 The children are taken back to their base class and remain there till the end of the day.

15.00 The last 30 minutes of the day are used by the teacher and helper for reflecting on the day and writing up the daily records. It has been found that the observational notes are more valuable because they are less incomplete and patchy when done together, which is probably because some children relate to one adult more than another. Twice a week staff are officially available to see parents but make themselves accessible at other times too. Trying to share what they do with parents is obviously valuable but it is a fine art to be welcoming to parents and yet not to let them monopolize the precious recording time five days a week.

The nurture group and the National Curriculum

The group curriculum is designed to provide the necessary developmental and formal experiences to enable children to overcome their emotional and behavioural difficulties and to be able to return to work with their mainstream class at a level appropriate to their age.

The ethos of the group is based on the principles elaborated by Marjorie Boxall in her pamphlet, *The Nurture Group in the Primary School* (see Chapter 2). It is very much one of working together and of building trusting and rewarding relationships. There is great emphasis on the relationships within the group, between children and between adult and child, and, as necessary role models, between teacher and assistant. Equally important are the relationships with all other members of staff, and with parents and outside agencies. It is recognized that it is the consistent and positive attitudes of the adults that build up the child's confidence and self-esteem.

In the group, the activities planned have to enable the child to experience through a structured programme the early learning developmental skills which they have missed. They must also fulfil the child's legal right to the National Curriculum (Enfield, 2000). These two strands, therefore, have to be kept in mind and brought together in a way which meets the individual needs of each child. As the children are all at different developmental and intellectual levels, the materials available must range from play equipment appropriate to a very early age to formal work material which they will meet in their mainstream class. Formal work will be differentiated to meet the child's needs so that children may be working at all levels from pre-curriculum to level 2 and in a few instances to level 3. This requires careful planning in cooperation with other staff, and recording and evaluation of the work done.

Including the foundation subjects as an integral part of the early learning experience has not been found to be difficult. Music, for example, as well as being fun is a shared experience and it enhances children's listening skills. In physical education, children can improve their gross motor control by using large nursery equipment, which makes it easier for them to manage PE in the school hall with their base class, where the group assistant will accompany them if necessary. In some schools arrangements are made for the group children to visit the school nursery to share the use of large toys and play equipment. Similarly, for literacy and numeracy, a regular slot might be negotiated with a mainstream class to use their computers when they are elsewhere. These visits not only fulfil curricular requirements but enhance the children's feelings of being part of the school. They also give them the experience, new to some, of an outing as in a family where attention has to be paid to the needs of other members of the group.

The importance of early play activities is much emphasized; the children, having usually missed out on 'mother's knee' experiences, need them to develop their natural curiosity. They must also be helped to understand the dynamics of group relationships, which have been beyond them in mainstream class. This emphasis does not mean that they lose out on the curriculum that is on offer to their mainstream classmates. A breakdown of the activities and resources found in nurture groups would show that they both encourage the essential development of early learning skills and also provide the National Curriculum core and foundation subjects. Cooking, for example, involves organizing, investigating, making choices, explaining, communicating, predicting, questioning and answering, taking turns, cooperation, fine motor control and visual motor coordination. These activities are part of the National Curriculum areas of language, mathematics, science and personal and social education. They are introduced at first through play which is structured in a way that allows a progression through the early learning stages which mainstream education takes for granted. As the children absorb the skills of self-management, they come to the stage where they can take responsibility for managing their work in a way appropriate to their age without the close supervision of the adults. Like good parents, the adults move the child on to the next stage as soon as he or she is ready.

Learning to relate

As all this learning is taking place, the children are being helped to overcome their relationship difficulties. By working through the stages of group membership, with adult support, they are coming to understand the rules which govern group acceptance which most children are assumed to have acquired by the time they reach school. Children in nurture groups have commonly not achieved these levels of competence and once they are settled in the group, the process of group acceptance will begin. This is often very tentative at first, with the adult observing and encouraging. A child may spend some time as an onlooker before beginning to join in alongside another child.

In working as one of a pair, the beginnings of cooperative play emerge. Then will come a phase of discovering ways in which they can become part of a larger group, working collaboratively as they begin to understand the rules for becoming a group member. The nurture group has constantly to create the opportunities for a child to work through these stages, with the adults commenting explicitly and positively on what is needed and on progress made. As they begin to receive acceptance from other members of the group they visibly grow in self-confidence and self-esteem and eventually as they consolidate these skills with the support of the adults they are ready to start the reintegration process.

Working with parents

It is part of Enfield's educational policy that from the beginning of a child's schooling steps should be taken to enable schools and parents to work together to ensure that the needs of each child are met. There is a 'Starting School' booklet, filled in by parents and teachers together, which gives parents the opportunity to learn about the school and to tell teachers facts about their child which will help in their education.

The 1993 Code of Practice supports such policies, with its stages for recognizing and meeting the child's educational needs which enable parents and school to share any concern. Enfield's response to the Code is their 'Record of Pupil Progress and Concern'. The Special Educational Needs Coordinator in each school has the responsibility of seeing that for children on the different stages of assessment, individual education plans and meetings with parents are kept up to date. Therefore, if a school with a nurture group feels that the appropriate help for a child in difficulties is to be placed in the group, there ought by that point to be a good relationship between school and parent.

There will need to be an opportunity for parents to discuss the ways in which the nurture group can help their child. Any early meeting must obviously be handled sensitively. After all, the nurture group's task is to take children through their missed early childhood experiences. If the meeting to explain this is mishandled, parents could be made to feel criticized and inadequate. Indeed, the name 'nurture group' might in itself be a threat to parents, and to avoid this the groups have different names such as the 'Rainbow Class'. This was an issue well understood by the ILEA schools, where 'nurture group' was intended to be used only as an administrative term, with each school having individual names by which their group was known. The difficulty in finding another generic term is that 'nurture' so exactly describes what the groups provide.

Working with parents of children with special educational needs can be time-consuming and difficult. In Enfield, with its commitment to involving parents as fully as possible in the education of their children, when the school suggests nurture group placement, the parents are usually already aware that their child is having difficulties and are pleased that extra help is available. At the meeting to discuss admission to the group, they will often volunteer considerable information about their child, the family and the home circumstances which helps the school to understand the child's difficulties better.

Other parents take longer to build up a relationship with the school. In some cases, fortunately very rare, parental attitudes are such that the efforts of the nurture group staff to explain the difficulties the child is having in school and the possibilities of group help are not accepted. For the sake of the child, staff must persevere because it is felt that in conflicts between school and home the child is invariably the loser. A child would not be placed in a group if the parent sustained their objection but this in fact has never arisen.

Once the child has joined the nurture group, parents are made to feel as welcome in the group room as does the child and so time is set aside for parents to discuss their child's progress regularly, as is required as part of the Code's Stage 3 review of progress. The nurture group staff are of course available to parents on open evenings but as always, for a variety of reasons, some parents do not use these opportunities. The nurture group staff are aware that some parents find it quite intimidating to come into school so they try to be as flexible as possible, encouraging parents to drop in informally, after the afternoon session, when the children have returned to their mainstream class, and providing other opportunities such as before school or at lunch time. They try to make these occasions as relaxed as possible by offering a cup of tea and a biscuit, by welcoming younger children, and by giving the parents time to talk.

If it becomes necessary for parents to see the educational psychologist for further assessment of the child's needs, which might result in special school placement, the nurture group room is often used for the meeting as it provides a familiar and non-threatening environment. If necessary the nurture group staff can be present to facilitate the discussion and provide support for parents.

Parents' attitudes: what research shows

An educational psychologist in training (Henson, 1994) studied parents' reactions to their child's placement in a nurture group. The majority were glad for the child to be offered the help but some had been hesitant when it was first suggested. Then the cooperation of the mainstream class teacher was important. One mother said that she felt upset at the suggestion but when she asked the class teacher if she would have let her own son join the group she was reassured. Parents generally felt that there was no stigma attached to being in the group. They were all glad of the help their children had received. Asked what they thought would have happened without a nurture group in the school, all would have predicted negative outcomes: 'I hate to think', 'He would have had to go to a special school.'

Placing children in a nurture group

Staff discussion

It cannot be emphasized too much that a nurture group has to have the support of the whole staff. Against such a background, the agreed Enfield LEA procedure for referrals to the nurture group works well. The child is discussed by the head teacher, class teacher, the nurture group teacher and the school's educational psychologist. Children are not usually considered for placement in the group until they have had a few weeks to settle in school. Then those who have not responded to ordinary class teaching and who are very restless, cannot listen, behave aggressively or impulsively or who are withdrawn and unresponsive will be considered. There are no absolute rules about which children will benefit most from a place; several factors have to be considered such as the composition of the group, discussed below, and alternative sources of help. As an Enfield head teacher says:

> This school has become very skilled at looking at children with special educational needs and choosing the right service. Children do not come in a mould; they are different. Some are shy and withdrawn, reluctant to come to school, cannot form relationships, cannot work alongside other children. Others know no boundaries in their behaviour; they dominate the class, are extremely demanding of adult attention, aggressive to other children, unable to share or cooperate with the class group. Others are something of a mystery to their teachers: they seem to be failing to mature emotionally or physically; they seem very vulnerable, they cannot become part of the class, they need help in mixing. They are not just 'naughty' children, nor children not achieving academically because of limited ability; nor children with difficulties caused by hearing or visual impairment or some other learning disability.

Consulting parents

When the staff decide that a child needs nurture group placement, the teacher who has the best relationship with the parents would be asked to discuss the suggestion with them, so that they are approached carefully and do not feel threatened. They are usually only too pleased that their child is being offered help. Staff in the school quoted will often already have a good idea of which children are likely to need extra help from observing them in the school toddler group. It might be a child whose parents seem overwhelmed, perhaps by several other younger children; or sometimes parents who seem to have a tenuous relationship with their child: there is little going on between them.

Also, parents may already know about the group from the school booklet which all schools provide to parents. One school's booklet contains the following:

> For a variety of reasons children might need extra help and support whilst at school to enable them to take full advantage of the curriculum. Occasionally we find that some children cannot cope with the demands of being in a full class, they may appear unsettled or distressed, and are unable to learn. After talking to the class teacher and the parents we may suggest that the child is admitted to 'Rainbow' class, where a teacher and a special welfare assistant work with a group of up to ten children, helping them to overcome their difficulties so that they will be able to resume their place in a full class situation as soon as possible.

The composition of the nurture group

A considerable body of expertise has been built up over the years in Enfield as in ILEA about what works best. It is agreed that it would not work for the group to be made up entirely of children with acting-out behaviour problems, nor of withdrawn, non-communicating children. A mix is needed. Then, other things being equal, the staff would give places to children judged most likely to be able to return to mainstream class. The expectation is that after three or four terms, with continuous monitoring to be sure their needs are being met, they should have developed the ability to stay on task, to work in a group and so to return to the mainstream class. Even if it is suspected that a child's difficulties are too severe for them to remain in mainstream in the long run, a place in a group might be offered because diagnosis of special needs in young children must almost always be tentative. The progress the child makes in the group might prove the original assessment to have been wrong.

Identification, assessment and monitoring

Identification of children needing the special help of a nurture group does not take place in a vacuum. It is part of an attitude to preventing children failing in mainstream education which has components drawn from national policy, from LEA policy and from the ethos of the individual school. A special educational needs policy which will include regular assessment and monitoring of children's progress is now recognized nationally to be essential for all schools, and the 1993 Education Act Code of Practice recommends appropriate structures. LEAs also have a role to play in helping schools to set their priorities and Enfield has responded to the 1988 and 1993 Education Acts by explicit policies for looking carefully at the needs of all children as they enter school which lead naturally to the identification of children with special educational needs.

First is the early involvement of parents in their children's school life. There is the 'Starting school' booklet, already described, to be completed by parent and teacher together which helps the parent to understand the school and gives the teacher valuable insights into the family background.

Secondly, there is a 'Baseline assessment' to be completed on a four-point scale for each child soon after entry to school which gives an 'Entry profile' of the child's level of skills in literacy and mathematics as observed by the teacher in the course of normal school activities.

Thirdly, suggested for use with children who score low on the baseline assessment, are guidelines to help teachers to look at aspects of the child's life which may be significant. These are

1. relationships,

2. health,

3. communication,

4. confidence and independence,

5. emotional development,

6. response to learning activities,

7. concentration and

8. coordination.

Any problems noted lead to an 'Action sheet' to help to plan appropriate help.

For children considered to have special educational needs there is a 'Record of pupil progress and concern' to be used in conjunction with a SEN audit form and in addition there are LEA forms for individual education plans.

Individual schools may have additional sources of information for identifying special needs. One Enfield head teacher said:

> The Borough puts a strong emphasis on home/school links. All primary schools were invited to bid for funding for some initiative in this area and this school chose to have a toddler group one afternoon a week, where parents come with their children. While the children play supervised by staff, parents can get support informally from each other, or more formally by staff talking about some aspect of school life. This might be dinner time arrangements, or parents' worries about bullying or some other topic. This contact means that by the time children join the school, either the nursery class or the first infant class, parents know the school, and through this early opportunity have had a positive experience. If it then becomes necessary to discuss concerns about the child's progress, the parents are likely to have started to build up some trust in the staff and so there is a good basis for discussion.

By the time a child reaches a nurture group therefore, its needs will be well documented and recorded in such a way as to pinpoint appropriate help. It is important also to have a baseline of the child's attainments and skills against which progress can be evaluated and regular time for staff recording and discussion. As has been noted, this takes place in the group itself daily, and once a term more formally with senior and support staff.

In addition to these records, the children's needs are also considered in the light of the Boxall Profile, discussed in Chapter 2, which is found by Enfield to be a valuable source of insight into children's difficulties as well as a means of monitoring their progress.

Reintegration

In Enfield, the authority's guidelines suggest that children should not need to spend more than four terms in a nurture group and that reintegration into the mainstream class is a central aim. Continued membership of the mainstream class is used positively through the relationship between the class teacher and the nurture group staff so that effectively the reintegration process starts when a child is first accepted for the nurture group. The child's parting from the class teacher and his or her return for the final part of each day is planned to be a positive experience, contributing to the child's feeling of being valued, of his or her life being predictable.

When the skills and attainments necessary for the child to fit back into mainstream class have been achieved, a decision to reintegrate will be made by the nurture group staff, the special educational needs coordinator, the head teacher and the school's educational psychologist, in consultation with parents and the mainstream teacher, and the return to mainstream will be negotiated carefully. For some children this will need to be very gradual, starting with just one session a week and building up slowly until the process is complete. Other children cannot wait to be back with their peers and for them reintegration takes place quickly. The level of their achievements will have moved towards the appropriate level for their age; indeed some children need integration into the mainstream class earlier than their overall state would suggest because they have moved on academically and need the stimulus of a better functioning peer group. In such cases they would be given some extra support in their mainstream class either from the nurture group staff or from other services.

The success of the operation depends on the child, on the support from parents, on the liaison which has been built up between the nurture group staff and the mainstream teacher; in short on the ethos which ensures that the returning child feels welcome.

Children for whom the nurture group is not enough

Although the proportion of children able to progress in mainstream as a result of nurture group placement is high, it cannot achieve this for all children. Occasionally children from very disturbed homes may respond to the nurture group approach for the few hours they are in school, but this cannot outweigh the damage done at home. If the home cannot be helped adequately by social work intervention, such a child might have to be found a substitute home, or be placed at a special school. The time spent in the nurture group will at least have helped to give a clearer picture of the source of the difficulties and of how better to meet the child's needs. Other children, to quote Marjorie Boxall:

> show markedly aggressive and vindictive behaviour that is calculated and is part well-organised but anti-social competence. This may be indicative of a problem that is too entrenched, particularly if the child is older, to respond sufficiently to nurture-work in a day setting. More information about the home situation is needed before a decision is made with the parents about the most appropriate form of help.

In Enfield, a minority of children continue to have special educational needs after a year or more in the nurture group. This does not mean that group placement has failed; some of these will have improved so much in their level of functioning because of their time in the group that they can be kept in mainstream class, albeit with some extra support. A few children will turn out to have such serious learning difficulties that they will need special provision. Again, this does not mean that nurture group placement has been a waste of resources. On the contrary, many parents, seeing their child valued and lovingly cared for with a great deal of individual attention, come to accept the painful reality of the extent of their disability. Everybody who works with children with serious learning difficulties knows the stress and cost of having to negotiate with angry parents. They may perhaps be unable to accept the extent of their child's disability, feeling that he or she has been consigned to special provision without a chance to succeed in mainstream.

While helping parents to come to terms with the reality of their child's condition is not the main purpose of the nurture groups, it is nevertheless a valuable function they sometimes perform. To give an example, a child with considerable neurological damage had been placed in a nurture group to see how much change could be effected with the extra help available there. At the review his parents agreed with the psychologist that, however much help he had had in the nurture group, he would need a more protected environment than a mainstream school could provide and they were able to comfort the nurture group staff who had hoped to achieve greater improvement. The support of senior staff and the educational psychologist becomes important is such situations. The nurture group staff may need to be reminded of how much worse the child would have been without the group's help.

Enfield's evaluation of nurture groups

Enfield LEA has consistently evaluated its nurture groups. A report compiled by the Educational Psychology Service in 1992 showed that the groups were effective as to outcomes and cost. A total of 203 children who had been placed in the groups since they began in 1984 were followed up. Of these, an impressive 88 per cent had remained in mainstream school. (Interestingly, Marjorie Boxall, monitoring the progress of ILEA children, arrived at a similar success rate.) The report also pointed out that costs in themselves were low compared with alternative provision, an effect enhanced both by the fact that a Statement of special educational need, itself an expensive procedure, was not required for placement, and further by the fact that the duration of placement was significantly shorter. In 1996, these findings were confirmed as is shown in Table 3.1.

Table 3.1 Costs of nurture groups compared with other special provision for pupils with EBD

---

1. Placement at EBD residential school: £20,000 to £60,000 per annum

2. Tuition for a statemented child from EBD support service:

(a)	2.5 hours weekly @ £27 an hour for 39 weeks	£2632.50 per annum
(b)	5 hours classroom assistant (est. post)	
	@ £9 an hour for 39 weeks	£1755.00 per annum
	(or CRA sessional post.....................................	£1267.50 per annum)

Annual cost per annum approx.......................... £4000

Average period of tuition is 3 years so average cost per child
(excluding cost of statement).............................. **£12,000**

3. Nurture group placement:
on average, child returns to mainstream class in less than a year, so 13 children are supported annually.

Staffing costs of group are £36,992 so average cost per child
.... **£2845.53**
(Provision is at Stage 3 of Code of Practice so there are no statementing costs)

Source: Report to Education Committee, Enfield, June 1996.

Comparative outcomes

Experiments on children's development are not often possible because of obvious limitations on what can be done to children in the cause of science. However, the chance to observe differences in progress, comparing like with like, occurred when two proposed groups, with 24 children identified for placement by agreed procedures, had to be cancelled because of financial cuts. Twenty of the children were able to be followed up, and their progress compared with 308 of the 425 children placed in groups in Enfield since their inception. This, reported in Iszatt and Wasilewska (1997), showed (Table 3.2) that the proportion of children in the control group requiring formal assessment and special provision was three times greater than in those children placed in groups. The proportion of children requiring special EBD school provision is almost seven times greater.

Table 3.2 Outcomes: A. Children assessed but not placed in NGs. B. Children placed in NGs

No. of children	Kept in main-stream	Kept in main-stream + Stage 3 support	Kept in main-stream + state-mented support	Moved to EBD day school	Moved to EBD residential school	Moved to other special school
A: 20	10 (50%)	1 (5%)	2 (10%)	2 (10%)	3 (15%)	2 (10%)
B: 308	255 (82.8%)	12 (3.9%)	8 (2.6%)	9 (2.9%)	2 (0.7%)	22 (7.1%)

Source: amalgamated from Appendix 6 and 7 in Report to Education Committee, Enfield, June 1996.

Assessment of special needs

It will be clear by now that there is a great commitment in Enfield to nurture groups and a belief that they are a valuable part of the LEA's Special Educational Policy. There is another, perhaps less obvious, advantage which is the sensitizing of the whole staff group to the needs of children. Schools that have nurture groups believe that the insights which they help to develop in all staff contribute to a better understanding of the learning needs of many other children which is relevant to the effective working of the formal procedures introduced by the 1993 Education Act Code of Practice.

This requires the progress of all children to be looked at systematically, so that those beginning to fail can be given special help. But the assessment of children in difficulties is not a simple matter. The aspects of progress that are chosen as significant and the way they are explained rely on assumptions about the causes of educational success and failure, which are often implicit rather than held up to scrutiny and staff discussion. The better understanding of child development engendered by nurture groups contributes to a more accurate assessment.

Attainments

Attainments in the basic subjects are obviously one important indicator of progress and since the 1988 Education Act all schools are required to assess these at various points in a child's school career. This is a necessary first step in identifying children who need extra help but it is by no means enough in itself. It is all too easy for busy teachers to equate attainments with ability and not to look for better potential. Some children will be somewhat behind the average for their age because their general ability is below the average. This is, however, not a conclusion that should be drawn without some supporting evidence and some reflection on other possible causes of poor learning.

It is obviously essential that quite common reasons for children's retardation are understood. Before it is assumed, for example, that a child who is slow to learn to read is of limited ability, it is important to make sure that he or she can see and hear properly and has had access to skilled and consistent teaching of literacy. Moreover, children may reach an average level of attainments and therefore not be causing concern. Yet they may be underfunctioning seriously because they are of high ability and should be working at a high level. In short, there are dangers in equating attainments and ability, and the measurement of attainments is only a starting point in assessing a child's progress.

Inappropriate behaviour

Another indicator of difficulties is a child's inability to behave acceptably, but again this cannot be looked at in isolation. Before valid judgements can be made about any one child, it is obviously important that the general level of behaviour in the school is acceptable, that there is an effective behaviour policy – a point made emphatically by the Elton Report (DES, 1989) and also by the Department for Education (1994a) in *Pupil Behaviour and Discipline*. After that, behaviour has to be seen in the context of the child's overall circumstances. A quiet child, causing no trouble, perhaps producing a minimum of work, may be underfunctioning badly and have serious emotional problems. A child may be behaving badly for reasons which, if his or her life situation is understood, are only too obvious and should not be ignored. It is important to look at the child with insight, not only at the surface behaviour. The National Curriculum Council as long ago as 1989 drew attention to the dangers of a superficial reaction to deviant behaviour in *A Curriculum for All*:

> For pupils with emotional/behavioural problems there are dangers in overemphasis on 'managing' the behaviour without attempt to understand the child's feelings... It may be important to assess, or seek expert advice about the extent to which the learning difficulties could be causing or contributing to behavioural problems or how much they are likely to be a consequence of such problems.

The 1993 Education Act has set up the necessary structures and LEAs, as Enfield demonstrates, can set the tone, give a lead, and issue prescriptive guidelines on how to monitor the progress of all children and how to help children who are in danger of failing. All of this is extremely important in helping to build a positive ethos, but a heavy responsibility still rests with the individual school. Assessment should be used in the context of a sound knowledge of barriers to good progress; procedures, however well intended, can, if used mechanistically, give dangerously misleading impressions.

School ethos

For assessment to work well, to lead to effective action, therefore, there needs first to be a school ethos which gives a high priority to helping children in difficulties, where staff discuss children's progress in constructive terms, are supportive of each other and, of course, where there are resources from which the assessed needs can be met. Secondly, teachers need an adequate understanding of all the factors that contribute to children learning well or badly. Lacking this, schools can go through the required motions of assessment without the educational chances of children being greatly enhanced.

What is necessary therefore is to create a positive climate of opinion towards children in difficulties. This is always important but particularly so when a significant proportion of children are coming into school from homes which are not able to support their education adequately. To achieve this, the leadership of the head teacher is paramount, as is a conviction that good teaching can be effective in helping seriously disadvantaged children.

One of the well-recognized benefits of the existence of a nurture group in ILEA schools was the contribution it made to the development in all staff of a professional understanding of the factors which influence progress in school. This was shown by the evidence given by ILEA head teachers to the Fish Committee, as discussed earlier. Enfield also recognizes this effect. As one of the head teachers there said:

> The ethos of the nurture group gets across to the rest of the school staff. This is for several reasons. First, there is a fairly stable staff group here, with not too many changes. Then the work of the nurture group is well

understood by all the staff. The teacher-tutor who organizes the induction of new staff spends time on explaining the group's work and function. The support of the whole staff group is of paramount importance, and involving them in discussions about which children should be placed in the group spreads a valuable understanding of all children's needs.

Good use of scarce resources

If scarce resources are to be used to the best advantage and if children are to be given appropriately structured help, there has to be an agreed way of assessing their needs. As well as this, since progress is now very properly required to be monitored regularly, their pattern of need has to be expressed in such a way that it can be reassessed and any change noted. There is no generally accepted scale for measuring emotional and behavioural difficulties. The Diagnostic Developmental Profile (now the Boxall Profile), described in the previous chapter, is used in Enfield, and in other schools where there are nurture groups, and is highly regarded.

The means it provides of looking at the behaviour in school of all children is found to give a framework for observing and understanding the child's behaviour; its use sharpens observational skills and provokes reflection on the causes of children's difficulties. It also provides a way of recording which allows easy comparison of changes over time, and an analysis of the child's behaviour which points to the compensatory experiences needed for progress to be made. It provides a consistent and easily scrutinized profile, in histogram form, which highlights the child's areas of need and gives some indication of the origins of the maldevelopment. It also provides a baseline for monitoring progress. In Enfield, for example, the child's profile is reviewed each half-term; changes which indicate the success of intervention or point to the need for other approaches are noted and individual education plans are then modified as necessary.

The head teacher of an ILEA junior school described the effect of its use in her school in the early 1980s:

> We gained a sort of positive language. To identify where a child is in different areas in its development was quite tough; there was no history, or training or background to doing that. It helped people to look more neutrally, or more perceptively, or think where does this behaviour come from. It put some structure into teachers' thinking and reporting.

Whatever the method of assessing the needs of children with emotional and behavioural difficulties, it is important that it should use and enhance the professionalism of staff and work to the benefit of the children.

Nurture groups in other forms and other places

So far we have drawn on the structure and organization of nurture groups in Enfield which closely follow those used in ILEA. But, as has been said, there was wide interest in nurture groups throughout the UK and they have been established not only as an integral part of mainstream schools but as special provision. Many special boarding schools for children with serious emotional and behaviour difficulties have found the nurturing approach of great help. One of its assets is that its rationale is easy for anyone with an intelligent interest in children to understand.

Its ideas speak to everybody's experience so that they are easily grasped by people without much formal training, which, as the Warner Report published by the Department of Health (1992) makes clear, is the case with many staff in residential social work. The nurturing approach encourages adults to see deviant behaviour as having its roots in the lack of a constructive and affectionate learning environment in the early years. This leads to compassion for the child, a very necessary quality in view of the appalling behaviour that disturbed children can present, and at the same time to a conscious plan to provide healthy experiences to help the child to grow through their negative feelings and attitudes.

As well as the ILEA/Enfield model of the nurture group, which receives children only from the school where it is based, there have been other arrangements. Writing in 2000, there is great interest in different forms of nurture groups. Many of the students on the Cambridge Certificate Course, for example, are running Pupil Referral Units, which are off-site and entirely for pupils excluded from mainstream school. Other LEAs are considering setting up nurture groups as an area resource. It is therefore helpful to be able to read of this form of provision in Newcastle upon Tyne.

The Newcastle Experience of Nurture Groups 1985–1996

Keith Hibbert, Mary McDonald, Willie Muir and David Simpson

Two nurture groups were formed in Newcastle upon Tyne in 1985. They were based in adjoining infant and junior schools on a council estate to the north of the inner city, renowned for its high levels of unemployment, vandalism and crime. The infant and junior schools later merged to form one primary school. The school population consists mainly of children from single-parent families of low income. As an indicator of social position, 80 per cent of the current roll of 256 (plus 52 in a full-time nursery) receive free school meals.

The units were established as LEA provision with the intention that they would serve the needs of children from other city schools, as well as from the host school. This challenges many of the precepts of the nurture group as we had come to know them from visits to ILEA schools and from meetings with Marjorie Boxall. It also immediately raised other questions. Could the units work as nurture groups on this basis? Had we chosen the right schools? How would the staff receive them? What would be the response of the other schools to their own children once they were placed outside the home school?

The commitment of our teachers and psychologists to the concept of nurture was clear. We understood the psychological sense of providing compensatory sustaining experiences to children whose difficulties were apparent on entry to school, whether through lack of effective early socializing experiences, or for reasons not yet apparent which a nurturing environment would help define. We could see an opportunity to work more intensively and more effectively with parents. We could see the value to a whole school of providing something which in its nature was so fundamental to children's needs, yet so rare an opportunity for teachers that it might, by its very existence, nurture staff and children alike. We knew that to be successful, this needed to be a whole-school venture, yet the school, which by any criteria could have made full use of its own nurture group, had to receive more children with similar needs from a wider group of schools. Could it work? The groups have now survived into the mid-1990s and an account of our experience may help others contemplating similar developments.

A review of special educational provision

At the time of the formation of the nurture groups in Newcastle, the LEA was conducting a review of its special educational provision in the wake of the introduction of the 1981 Education Act. The needs of all children presenting 'difficult to manage' behaviour were high on the list of concerns in the city. At the time there was no provision based in mainstream, and the future plan contained a proposal to close one special school for 'maladjusted' children and to utilize the funding to create some unit provision in the primary and secondary sectors. The educational psychologists were asked to contribute to planning by advising the LEA on the nature, range and causes and the means of managing emotional and behaviour difficulties.

In the course of preparing advice, the psychologists became increasingly aware of the extent of need for specialist support and provision among young children of infant school age and below. A visit to Newcastle by David Weikart, the founder of High/Scope in the USA, combined with visits to ILEA nurture groups by the principal educational psychologist and a group of interested teachers, reinforced a growing conviction that our investment should be in provision in the early years. We thought that our need was for a unit which took account of the overall needs of children – social, emotional and cognitive – and therefore with an ethos as close as we could get to the successful nurture groups we had seen.

We were aware that the ILEA nurture groups existed exclusively for the school's own use. We were persuaded that the methodology and rationale were right for the needs of many of our inner-city children. But our schools could not individually afford to develop the provision, and so a decision was made to establish the groups in Newcastle as LEA rather than individual school provision.

Getting started

It was not difficult to obtain the support of either the education committee or its officers for the establishment of our provision. The principle was readily agreed: to establish two nurture groups in mainstream schools at infant and junior levels. But introducing and holding on to the concept of nurture has sometimes been a challenge.

Where to locate the units

The location of the units was the first question. Should they be in schools in an area of high social deprivation, where staff were already challenged by the extent of learning and behaviour difficulties in their own population and the implications of this for role models among other children? Or should they be in a setting with at least one head teacher whose management skills, vision of the role of the school and positive enthusiasm for the concept of the nurture groups would provide a strong platform for their establishment? This factor in the end ruled the day and determined where the groups would be located. The decision did not remove the challenges of establishing two units in adjoining infant and junior schools with head teachers whose views proved to be very different, which created problems in working together for the two nurture group staffs. Nor did we anticipate the merger of the two schools within the first two years of the groups' lives. There was also the problem of staff feelings about the establishment of the units and the implications for them of additional work and stress.

The LEA or the school's provision?

The most significant challenge to the establishment of a nurturing ethos was the question of whose resource they were. The groups were set up as LEA provision with a brief to provide for a wider population than that of the host schools. The schools themselves, however, had more than enough children to fully occupy the staff of the units. They also had the task of establishing the provision successfully in the schools, of securing staff support and participation, of appointing staff, of identifying a suitable central location in the building – in short, of managing all aspects of this change.

An example of the potential conflict of interest arose early on around the question of the timing of admission of children from other schools. The head teachers had established with the LEA the principle that for some time the units should be permitted to establish themselves by catering for the populations of their own schools. As always, unforeseen issues arose which delayed the establishment of stability in the groups, and so the heads sought to extend the transitional period. LEA officers faced contrary pressures from elected members and from other head teachers interested in using the new provision. This issue took many hours of discussion to resolve and highlighted a significant tension in managing an LEA provision of this kind. Nor was it the only question requiring resolution; questions soon arose about funding, staff appointments, admissions criteria and procedures, and many other issues.

The questions were resolved due to the willing and widely representative management group which was established for the two units. It is clear, however, that issues that arise from the establishment of groups as LEA rather single-school provision, while they can be resolved, create a layer of significant additional management tasks which demand time and energy.

Gaining whole-staff support

We had returned from studying nurture groups in London with a clear view that nurture was a function of the whole staff, not just of the teachers in the groups, and that this was crucial to the success of the groups. The task was to establish a nurturing ethos throughout the school as a solid basis for all education. We had to persuade the staff that placing the provision in their school would benefit them and the school as a whole. While the children referred to the units would cause extra work because they would need a base in their classes, the whole school would have the advantage of:

- the support of the nurture group staff who would have time programmed for work in their classes;
- the ability to refer children who might benefit to the nurture groups, an immense source of support to individual teachers to be able to share their concerns and to gain some respite;
- the existence of the provision which would help to shape the ethos of the school and draw in expertise to help the development of positive school systems. In the early days, much work was done with all teachers to establish a screening procedure to help staff to identify the most vulnerable children, and a training and consultation framework to support staff throughout the school.

It is easier in some respects to establish good practice than to maintain it. In the enthusiasm of establishing this new venture, much ground was gained through the effort and good will of all staff. As time has gone by, demands have increased and resources have diminished. Maintaining principles, practice and ethos has been demanding, and the school has inevitably had to adapt to the changes around it.

The Boxall model

The units were initially established to operate closely in line with the principles of nurture groups as outlined by Marjorie Boxall. They were given central and prominent locations within their respective schools. Whole-staff involvement was secured. Nurture group staff devoted time to the support of other teachers in the school. Children were expected to remain in the groups for a short time (up to a maximum of 18 months) and on a flexible part-time basis, each child having a class base elsewhere in the school. The groups nurtured their children's development and socialization – they accepted, supported, fed, listened to and provided play experiences with their children. An advisory group of school and LEA staff (officers, psychologists and senior advisers) was established to support the groups themselves to develop: define their boundaries, help to maintain them, support their quest for resources and help in the evaluation of the work.

The units were originally established to offer a new opportunity to children who were experiencing emotional, behavioural, social and learning difficulties which might threaten the success of their placements in mainstream classrooms. Children on placement in the units would still access mainstream teaching, National Curriculum and national assessment, but this would always be tailored to individual needs. When in class, if a unit child was seen to have some difficulty, he or she might be withdrawn to the unit, talked through the problem or concern and be reintroduced to the larger class when he or she was thought to be ready.

The nurture groups in 1996

From application to placement

When a school applies for a placement in the nurture groups, it is assumed they have gone through all the Code of Practice stages of support, and have exhausted all their in-house resources for the child. An application is made, with relevant reports to the LEA whose Assistant Education Officer then approaches the school. Then begins the process of determining the suitability of placement. The teacher member of the unit pays a visit to the applying school to observe the child in class. A report is subsequently written and submitted with all other reports to an admissions meeting. All involved outside agencies are invited, e.g. the referring school's head and class teacher, educational psychologist, social services, child and family guidance service, health service. Parents will have had the opportunity to visit the unit informally prior to the referral being made, to meet staff and to reassure themselves about the provision and general ethos of the unit and school, and that they and their child would be happy with the placement. They are not invited to attend the admissions meeting.

The aim of the meeting is to determine a child's suitability for placement in relation to established nurture group criteria. All reports are considered and a recommendation on the suitability of the applicant is forwarded to the AEO for approval. An admission date is agreed, the parents are informed and pre-placement visits are set up for the child and parents as a phasing-in measure.

The placement is usually offered in the first instance on a term's 'assessment' basis, and is reviewed before the end of the three months. At this stage the assessment place is either extended, or the placement is confirmed. Further review meetings are held on a three-monthly basis and all interested parties are invited to them. In order to ensure the success of the placement, it is essential that parents and feeder school are involved throughout the period of the placement.

The role of the coordinator

Coordinating the work of the nurture groups is one of the roles of the school's special needs coordinator. It includes:

- daily management of the nurture groups;
- arrangement of referral and appropriate review meetings;
- liaison with outside agencies and the LEA;
- liaison between unit and mainstream staff;
- development and maintenance of a whole-school approach to the nurture groups;
- curriculum development to ensure National Curriculum differentiation to suit the needs of children in the groups;
- staff development;
- outreach visits as children succeed and need to move on;
- support to unit children in mainstream classes on a planned basis.

At first a newly placed child spends almost 100 per cent of the time in the unit with a gradual introduction to the mainstream class, fully supported by unit staff. By the end of the placement, the child will be spending most of the school day in a mainstream class with little or no support. A typical day in the group is very similar to that in the Enfield groups except that the unit children from across the city arrive at 8.45 by transport provided by the

LEA. They are met by a unit member of staff and join with the school's own unit children.

Change over time

Despite its undoubted success, the host school has experienced difficulties in maintaining the nurturing ethos over the ten years since the groups' inception. Changes in educational practice at national, local and school levels have all had an impact. There is a significant increase in demand for a variety of special educational provision for children who present disturbing patterns of behaviour or emotional development, an increase paralleled in other metropolitan LEAs in Britain. This has been accompanied in Newcastle, as elsewhere, by a decrease in available funding. The impact of these factors on the nurture groups and the host school is briefly discussed below.

Local management of schools (LMS)

The climate of financial management and the accountability of schools is now radically different from the time when the units were established. The school is accountable both to its governing body and to the LEA for the management of the school and its resources. The school's budget for 1994/95 is £527,768 from which £38,000 is allocated through the formula of additional weighting for the number of children receiving free school meals. The nurture group is a centrally held exception, separately funded by the LEA.

When the nurture groups were established, LMS did not exist. The issue of individual budgets targeted for specific need was not a priority. The school now has responsibility for the day-to-day management of the units. It manages referrals, liaises with other professionals and referring schools, is responsible for personnel and other unit management issues, provides a thorough response to the LEA about each referred child, and organizes all reviews. The school provides clerical support and the classroom bases with all their overheads.

There has been no increase in unit funding but in the past the school has had access to the unit for its own children. When the units were first established, the school was permitted to keep half of the unit's places for its own children, compensating for the administrative and organizational work of the school. This is no longer the case.

Budget constraints over the years have led to increased class sizes throughout the school, from average sizes of 23 in 1985 when the units were established, to 30 in 1996. This has created greater difficulty in supporting places for unit children in mainstream classes and raises questions for the host school about the need for enhanced resourcing. The existence of LMS has raised, but not yet resolved, the question of double funding, where children are already funded through the formula in their own schools and then come to the school to which the unit is attached either in the middle of the year, or for a short term or assessment place.

The pattern of demand for places

The type of referral has changed. Children have been referred with special educational needs who require provision beyond that which the nurture groups can reasonably supply. It is the only provision of its kind in the city, and has been approached when special schools have been full. This has threatened the identity of the nurture groups as an early preventive and supportive provision. Because the unit now has children with more extreme problems than in the past, the school no longer takes the view that unit children should be integrated into ordinary activities at play and lunch times and now provides children in the unit with access to their own playground in order to avoid disruption and conflict. Not only does this change of emphasis carry resource implications, but it marks a significant shift away from the whole-school nurturing ethos.

The number of children referred to the units has increased and with it has come an increase in the volume of administration to process them. This has placed greater demands on the Special Needs Coordinator.

Maintaining a positive working relationship between units and staff in the mainstream classes of the host school has become more difficult. Providing support from unit staff to mainstream staff has proved difficult when there has been a wide age range among unit children, requiring links with several teachers. Unit and mainstream staff must meet to plan individual education plans for unit children. Staff who are already faced with typical daily inner-city problems and with less support than before may see unit children, when they join mainstream classes, as added demands on their already stretched strategies and resources.

Originally there was no need for a statement of special educational need for children to be placed in the units. Now, a child may be placed with or without a statement. The school is concerned at a trend towards a growing number of children with statements of special educational need who are referred to the units. Under the Code of Practice a priority may be to renegotiate the position of this provision within the overall scheme of the LEA.

Retaining its special character

Since their inception, the nurture groups in Newcastle have had to respond to the kind of demands outlined above. These changes challenge the distinctive identity of the groups – conceptually and organizationally.

A distinctive approach

In the booklet, *The Nurture Group in the Primary School* by Marjorie Boxall, it was emphasized that the work done in nurture groups is not psychotherapy but essentially an educational approach employing skills at an early developmental level. In Newcastle, developing an operational definition of 'educational approach' has evolved over time to provide a balance of study, practice, play and practical activity. The methodology has been distinctive in the face of a growing need to support children with more extreme needs in the groups and the school as a whole. With such a set of demands there exists the risk that managing children's difficult behaviour predominates at the expense of what Boxall refers to as 'the early and intimate physical contact between adult and child, the warmth and intimacy of the family atmosphere and the good humoured acceptance with control of infantile and resistive behaviour'.

Nurture group work is a distinctive approach whose aims and methods must be recognized, accepted and protected. In Newcastle where only two groups exist in one school, opportunities for the training of staff have been rare, and opportunities more limited for teachers to share and develop practice with others. The professional isolation which can result places at risk the process of staff recruitment and retention.

A distinctive set of referral criteria?

The diagnostic criteria suggested by Boxall have provided important starting points for our groups. Helpfully she suggested that consideration is given to the extent to which 'a child can constructively engage in the day-to-day life of the class because of inadequacies which seem crucially linked with impoverishment and crippling in the early years'. Boxall acknowledges that the problems cover a wide spectrum of need and include children who are unresponsive and uncommunicative, as well as those who are violently aggressive and disruptive. In spite of their usefulness, the Boxall criteria have rarely been systematically used in making decisions about the appropriateness of a child's placement. There have been occasions where the pressure on the LEA and others to fund provision has been the dominant force. The absence of clearer criteria, together with the pressing needs of children have, therefore, sometimes combined to make consistent decision-making more difficult for the admissions panel.

Boxall has talked about nurture groups as flexible resources so that at the unit school children, because of problems of accurate prediction, have increasingly been admitted initially for a period of further assessment. Increasingly information is being provided about the nature and extent of a child's behavioural difficulties together with curricular strengths and weaknesses. There is a need, however, to reconsider the quality of information which is available and its relevance to the true work of a nurture group. Notwithstanding the need for clearer criteria it is noteworthy that very few children who have been admitted have later been deemed inappropriately placed.

A distinctive form of provision?

In spite of all the recent difficulties, the nurture groups throughout their existence have provided an invaluable resource in meeting the needs of a very vulnerable group of young children. Staff understand the philosophy behind them and have worked to ensure their success. The place of a nurture group should, however, be viewed in the context of a continuum of provision. Within this continuum it would then be possible more clearly to set out for each school or unit the range of special needs that provision has to meet. Newcastle LEA has identified significant gaps in its special provision, in part leaving the nurture group potentially vulnerable as the only resource for young children with emotional and behavioural difficulties, where an integral mainstream link is crucial. It is precisely under such circumstances that the distinctive character of such a group can begin to be eroded and the ability of all concerned to match needs to provision more accurately is significantly reduced.

Distinctive responsibilities?

Clarity of responsibility within schools and at LEA to school level for decision-making has remained a significant issue since the nurture groups were set up. The concept of shared responsibility for the individual programming of children has always been a central tenet; perhaps it became more formalized with the advent of the National Curriculum and is certainly now very much reinforced by the 1993 Education Act. Time for planning has to be 'paid' for and is an increasing need and cost to the school. Within the nurture group there are currently children at Code of Practice Stage 3 (i.e. those who benefit from such provision but who do not have a statement of special educational needs), children at Stage 4 (i.e. those children currently undergoing statutory assessment), and children at Stage 5 (i.e. those children who have a statement of special educational needs). There is now an urgent need for the responsibilities of the host school and the LEA to be clearly delineated with regard to the nurture group from both a management and financial viewpoint.

The nurture group has a proven track record in returning children unsupported back into mainstream schools. If it is to continue to do this it must keep its identity clear, with its aims and methods clearly understood. Some children have behavioural problems that need different provision, so fitting the group into the City's overall plan for special education is inevitably a complex matter. But the success of the approach since 1985 convinces us that the effort is worthwhile.

Chapter 4

Responding to Children's Needs

Marion Bennathan

Talking to nurture group staff past and present, reading accounts of their work in a privately circulated handbook, *Nurture: Principles in Practice in Ilea Nurture Groups*, the excitement of the work, the use it makes of teachers' and helpers' insights and inventiveness comes across most powerfully. Children in serious difficulties in school, living in homes which cannot give them the care most families take for granted, are helped to make such significant progress that they not only remain in mainstream school but develop positive attitudes to themselves and others which will affect their lives profoundly. The purpose of this chapter is to reflect on the normal pre-school learning such children will have missed and the ways in which nurture group teachers and helpers make this good.

It is easy for professional educators to underrate the amount of learning that goes on in ordinary homes. Most children come into school already having absorbed quite elaborate language skills, the necessary basis for the development of literacy and also, less obviously, for developing mathematical skills which start with an understanding of language-based concepts such as number, size, area and sequence. Most children have also learned to play alongside other children, and in so doing have developed the social and relationship skills necessary for the great move from life at home to life in a large group, where adult attention has to be shared and other children have to be considered.

Nurture group children, typically, have not had this good pre-school education as the descriptions below of three of them, two from London, one from Newcastle, will demonstrate.

Three children

Darren

Darren was six and a half. Before entering the nurture group, his teacher wrote:

> In school he cannot share and cannot play with the others without fighting. He is aggressive to teachers and to other children, swears, kicks and bites and refuses to cooperate. He has temper tantrums after which he

sits looking sullen and is vicious to other children. He seems to feel that nobody likes him and everyone is against him. He has moments of being perfectly charming but these are short-lived and he will quickly behave wildly, cannot sit in his chair, fights and disrupts everybody's work. His teacher tries to make contact by praising his work when this is possible but his reaction to this is to tear the work up and to run round the room, out of control.

At home, Darren's father takes no interest in the children. He beats his wife and the children witness violent fights. His mother is concerned about her children but her control is punitive. If Darren misbehaves, his clothes are taken away and he is kept in all weekend. He is made to sit in the bath for an hour at a time. He has almost no toys.

Darren settled well in the nurture group and most of the time was helpful and well behaved, enjoyed playing and making junk models, but had temper tantrums a few minutes before it was time to go home. Development was a series of ups and downs with episodes of violent and dangerous behaviour and tantrums followed by periods of calm. After about two months, silly and rude behaviour was mixed with concern and thoughtfulness for his teacher. His trust of people was still limited and he still had wild fits when his work was praised. He could not accept being refused a second biscuit, had a tantrum and cried and sobbed. He was not settled and not happy at school, although he would rather be there than at home.

After one term he was greatly improved and only had three or four tantrums in half a term. The composition of the group had changed and he now became the leader. He calmed down, seemed to feel wanted and needed and talked freely about himself. He seemed much happier but still some-times had the feeling that everyone was against him, and his teacher felt that the outcome of his placement in the group was uncertain. At this time his mother was in hospital, and after a violent tantrum when he was asked to give another child a turn on the scooter he sobbed, put his arms round the teacher and for the first time she felt that he knew that she cared for him.

Following this he steadily improved in his behaviour and work and in his interest in the world around him. He took on a lot more responsibility at school and at home and two terms after admission to the group was helpful and polite, and showed caring for the teacher and the other children. After three terms a new and very aggressive boy came into the group. Darren commented, 'I used to be a bit like that' and did not seem to like what he saw. He was put back into his ordinary class as it was feared he might be disturbed by the aggressive behaviour, and was said to be 'marvellous'.

He remained in the infant school for one more term and transferred without difficulty to the junior school. Five terms after leaving the nurture group, he was described as charming and well-liked by his teacher who found him very helpful and cooperative, 'thoroughly nice'. He played well with the other children and had a fantastic sense of humour.

Stacey

Stacey was five and a half when she was suggested for nurture group placement. Her teacher wrote:

> She will hardly speak to anyone apart from a grunt or a 'Yes' or 'No'. She does not play with other children and cries most of the time with sobs shaking her whole body. She constantly sucks two fingers, which she puts into her mouth up to her knuckles, while with her other hand she twirls the hair on top of her head. She makes no progress with her work. She appears to have no confidence, will not attempt anything new and cries if her teacher raises her voice slightly or even if she just looks cross.

Stacey's mother was deserted by her father and the family had to live in unsatisfactory temporary accommodation for over a year. When they were re-housed, her father returned to the family but was violent to her mother who went to live elsewhere, leaving the children behind with their father.

Stacey joined the nurture group towards the end of her second term in school. At first she cried almost all the time and seemed a very sad child, greatly in need of personal attention. For the first three months she followed the teacher around, wanting to sit on her knee and be with her the whole time. She needed to be rocked like a baby, arms round the teacher and head on her shoulder. When she played with the other children, however, she began to laugh and talk and seemed happier, but always started to sob and suck her fingers when the teacher made a simple request. She continued to need a great deal of attention and for a long time the need seemed insatiable.

Gradually the teacher became more firm with her and after about two terms she seemed much better. She was still sucking her fingers but far less often and when she cried it was usually because she was not getting her own way. The nurture teacher continued to be firm but gentle. Gradually Stacey improved a great deal, talked much more and settled down in the group. She worked well, would attempt new and difficult work and made a great deal of progress. She was now playing well with the others and only in moments of stress still sucked her fingers.

After three terms she returned to her ordinary class. A follow-up one year later indicated that she was playing and working well and seemed quite happy, though sometimes in moments of stress she sucked her fingers.

Five terms after she left the group and had moved to the junior school she was said to be settled, happy, always smiling and playing well with the other children. She was progressing well with her work, was confident with her teachers, did not cry when they were cross with her, and is now able to laugh at herself.

Margaret

Margaret was four when she was admitted to the nurture group. She had been physically and sexually abused from the age of two. She lived with her single mother who had social, emotional and financial problems, had been through the care system as a child and had attended special school; she was threatening and aggressive to Margaret and to nurture group and school staff. A younger brother was also suspected of having been abused by the same perpetrator who had since been imprisoned.

Margaret was screened in the nursery and assessed as suitable for placement. She bullied other children constantly, was aggressive to peers and staff, swore, shouted and actively encouraged other children into simulating sexual acts. Her language was of a sexual nature. She was totally undisciplined most of the time. She knew no boundaries. Her learning capabilities could not be assessed because her behaviour caused such anxiety that she was unmanageable. She was referred as an emergency to the nurture group where her placement proved to be successful. This was attributed to referral at an early age by the nursery. Next, her mother was persuaded to support the group programme by actively participating in it. The group became a 'home from home' to mother, who learned to smile, to share Margaret's success and show pride in her daughter, to share her own concerns about Margaret with group staff, and to take full advantage of all support services on offer. Margaret responded to the individual plan set by the group staff and supported by mother. All support agencies worked together well and Margaret and her mother discovered self-esteem they never thought they had or 'deserved'.

After the two-year programme, Margaret was reintegrated successfully into full-time mainstream. She can still be difficult at times and often has 'trying' periods but all support services are confident of her future success.

It will be clear that children with such experiences come into school in no state to work at a stage appropriate to their age. This chapter will look briefly at the learning that goes on in most ordinarily loving families and at the educational deficits children are likely to have without this background. It will also look at how nurture group staff work with the children to make up for their lack of good experiences, helping them to overcome their difficulties in relating to adults and to other children, and creating the sort of atmosphere which gives the intellectual stimulus and the teaching that is part of life in more supportive homes.

Language and progress

It is accepted that the good development of language is central to educational progress, closely connected with the acquisition of literacy, but language is also important in helping children to understand their world emotionally and socially, in helping them to internalize ideas of order and predictability. If they can explain themselves, express their feelings, they feel much more in control of what happens to them. Language is also about emotional communication: its use contributes to the quality of relationships. Words are used to comfort, to reassure. Any family has its comfort phrases with which to cushion the demands of reality, 'Just once more and then no more'. Morality is conveyed by the use of language, children proudly repeating the injunctions they have learnt. Says Emma, aged 2 and a half, 'Granny, you must learn to share, because sharing is good'.

Children express their understanding of the world verbally, practise behaviour and rehearse reactions. Sally, aged 2 and a half, stands in the park playground as a smaller child is climbing on to equipment she had been moving towards. She glares at him ferociously, and gestures him away sternly and repeatedly until he takes fright and retreats. Mother, who was preoccupied with the baby some distance away, comes up and says that that was not a very kind thing to do. Sally, in a deep and melodramatic voice, says, with every evidence of being pleased with herself, 'I am very horrible'. On a later occasion, she sits hunched on the sofa, and tells her grandmother that there is a notice on the door which says 'No aminals allowed in here'. Grandmother reads the imaginary notice, joins her on the sofa and asks which aminals we are keeping out. 'It's the dinosaurs in the garden. Their footprints make such a mess on the carpet.' Through such talk and play children are developing ways of managing their world, experiencing and internalizing control, making anxieties bearable. In the life of adequately nurturing families the opportunities for this are plentiful.

Some families cannot provide the conditions in which children can explore their environment in a way that furthers their development. It should be stressed that this is not a matter of social class, whose influence on language acquisition and forms of use considerably shaped research in the 1970s. It may well be true that, as Bernstein wrote in 1970:

the class system has affected the distribution of knowledge. Historically and now, only a tiny proportion of the population has been socialised into knowledge at the level of the metalanguages of control and innovation, whereas the mass of population has been socialised into knowledge at the level of context-tied operations.

These are important ideas and research on class differences in language development played its part in making people more sensitive to the many factors that make for educational success or failure, but it is not what we are concerned with here. Indeed the emphasis put on examining class differences in the development of language skills may have diverted attention from the amount of teaching of language that goes on in any ordinary home, whatever its social class, and therefore of the contribution made by pre-school experience to the acquisition of literacy.

Children vary quite widely in the age at which they start to produce recognizable words but, short of horrendous trauma or sensory deprivation, most are able to name objects and put words together by the time they are two or 2 and a half. By the third or fourth year, children move from what Blank and Solomon (1969) have usefully called the 'What?' to the 'Why?' stage. Children absorb some knowledge about their physical world, the here and now, just by seeing it, and in these days of universal television there is plenty to see. Naming things is an early stage of language development and most homes, even the most uncaring, will provide the conditions for this development. But the understanding of what is not visually present requires something more; the acquisition of more elaborate concepts, ideas of time, of sequence, of consequence, of causality, of predictability, depend on the intervention of an adult. Blank demonstrated that specific language tutoring of children from deprived backgrounds can improve their language concepts and hence their measured intelligence. Parents, tuned in to the child's stage of understanding and with a strong commitment to their progress, are well placed to listen, to explain, to link what the child says to other matters already understood. New concepts are introduced, received concepts are elaborated.

By the age of three, well-nurtured children are showing evidence of understanding sequences, of changes as time goes by. The philosopher, Bertrand Russell, is reputed to have said, 'Today is yesterday's tomorrow.'

Says Sally to her grandmother, 'What were you before you were Daddy's mummy?'

Says Joe cheerfully and affectionately, 'When I can look after myself, you'll die, won't you, Mummy?'

They not only have a sense of time, of sequence, they are beginning to make plans, showing that they feel themselves to have some choice and some control.

James, in Paris on holiday, when the Ribena had run out, said sternly, 'If I had known you couldn't get Ribena in Paris, I would never have left Birmingham.'

Sally announces her plans for the future. Having learnt to turn off a dripping tap, she is going to be a plumber; she is also going to be an author who will write 'wonderful stories for children and for grown-ups'.

In a loving home, moreover, children can reveal the imperfect state of their understanding without the criticism or ridicule that they might fear in school. Indeed, their mistakes are often admired as showing how much they have understood, which creates an excellent opportunity for further learning.

Clara aged two, watched her grandmother applying cosmetics to her hair.

'What you doing, Ganny?'

'Putting stuff on my hair.'

'Why?'

'To make me look pretty.'

'Why?'

'Because I'm going out tonight.'

Wrinkling up her nose in disgust: 'I not put that stuff on my hair.'

'Perhaps when you're a Granny you will.'

Clara, triumphantly, 'When I a Ganny, I'll be big and you'll be little.'

Grandmother left it to the parents to explain her mistake.

Pamela, aged almost four, was 'helping' her mother at the sewing machine on which pyjamas were being made for her father.

'Don't forget to leave a big hem so that you can let them down when he grows,' says Pamela.

'But Daddy isn't going to grow any more, darling,' says mother.

A thoughtful pause and then Pamela asks, 'Why does he eat, then?'

Mother is delighted at Pamela's reasoning ability.

Most families can recall such stories.

Two four-year-olds: 'But Mummy why does Daddy have to pay all these taxes? He always uses the car.'

'I shall buy you a big present, Mummy, when I go to school to earn.'

In an ordinarily supportive family, such errors lead to the refinement of concepts: the workings of the national economy, the differences (and connections) between earning and learning.

Children come to school with language skills and concepts at very different levels; some of which may be due to differences in innate ability, some because of different learning experiences. They therefore need opportunities to develop their language skills by listening and responding in an atmosphere where they feel at ease. Children in class who fail to understand most of what is said to them, for whatever reason, whether because of delayed development, undiagnosed hearing loss, emotional preoccupation or from a conviction of their own incompetence, are likely to become alienated, depressed, withdrawn, inattentive, or perhaps hyperactive.

Tizard and Hughes (1984) in their *Young Children Learning*, splendidly demonstrated the complexity and richness of the learning of language in ordinary homes. Their research material was collected by recording what was actually said in the homes of a group of four-year-olds. They found that most parents talk to their children in ways precisely structured to the child's level of understanding: explaining, reinforcing, reminding, helping children to draw morals; in short a highly personalized educational programme. The great divide was not between the social classes, although there was some difference by class in the complexity of parental response, but between the wealth of language experience that was on offer in the homes compared with what went on in school:

> We became increasingly aware of how rich this environment was for all the children. The conversations between the children and their mothers ranged freely, ... the children discussed topics like work, the family, birth, growing up and death; they talked with their mothers about things they had done together in the past, and their plans for the future; they puzzled over such diverse topics as the shape of roofs and chairs, the nature of Father Christmas, and whether the Queen wears curlers in bed. ... A large number of the more fruitful conversations simply cropped up as the children and their mothers went about their afternoon's business at home – having lunch, planning shopping expeditions, feeding the baby.

In school the picture was different:

> When we came to analyse the conversations between these same children and their nursery teachers, we could not avoid being disappointed. The children were certainly happy at school, for much of the time absorbed in play. However, their conversations with their teachers made a sharp contrast to those with their mothers. The richness, depth and variety which characterised the home conversations was sadly missing. So too was the sense of intellectual struggle, and of the real attempts to communicate being made on both sides.

The authors do not deny the value of nursery education:

> nursery schools and classes provide an important means of support for hard-pressed parents, ... a secure and enjoyable environment in which

young children can play, and explore the wider social world beyond the home.

They felt, however, that 'professionals might learn from observing children talking to their parents at home'. When this research came out, it caused considerable consternation amongst language experts, if a certain amusement to those who worked with children and their families and were well aware that lively conversation between parents and children is not solely a middle-class phenomenon.

This demonstration of the way in which language is absorbed in the home has implications for the teaching of all young children because it shows the conditions under which children learn naturally. It is particularly relevant in work with children with delayed language skills, the cause of which may be that the child has not had reasonable opportunities for learning language at home. It therefore reinforced the nurture group belief that many children were failing in school not because of innate incapacity but because they had not had the massive educational input from home that schools had taken as given (or indeed had hardly been aware of).

A further implication is that if school is to begin to make good these deficits, teachers and helpers have not only to be aware of the importance of helping the child's language development, they also have to be able to create the conditions of a good home. They have to have the time to build up an individual relationship with each child, time to observe the state of their understanding, an intimate knowledge of the child's current activities and interests, and the determination to use the ingenuity of a good parent to feed all of this into fostering the child's use of language. They have to create the safe setting where a child can reveal his or her ignorance without fear of blame or shame.

Barbara Maines, an educational psychologist working in a special school for children with emotional and behavioural difficulties, made some interesting discoveries about the level of children's understanding of spoken language. She noticed that a highly successful teacher habitually took great care to check that his pupils had understood what he asked them to do. He did not simply ask, 'Do you understand?' since he felt it was asking a lot of a child to answer a teacher in the negative. The teacher checked the child's understanding by asking such questions as, 'Will you explain to me what you are going to do now?'

Maines and Robinson (1991) decided to test the children's understanding of spoken language. This was found to be significantly lower than average, and well below the children's scores on the verbal items of standard intelligence tests. This makes one think that the children were not failing to understand the meaning of words so much as failing to be able to do so while relating to others; which leads to speculation on the complex connections between the understanding of language and the existence of 'emotional and behavioural difficulties'.

Helping language development

The relaxed atmosphere in the nurture group room, the implicit permission and active encouragement to play, are an important part of the opportunities the group provides to make good delayed development. Using language more fully and more precisely is one of the obvious gains, as the children discuss what they are doing with an interested adult who does what any good mother does: feeds back what the child has said in a supportive and extended form. As well as this constant, informal teaching of language, there are many other strategies. One group, to encourage language development, makes the class tape recorder available to the children throughout the day. They each have a tape of their own on which they can record comments. These conversations can be shared with one of the staff at a convenient time and often give an insight into what is going on in the child's life, their thoughts, their feelings – which is a help to staff in planning individual educational programmes.

One child has shown a particular skill at working with the computer. He is some three to four years behind in his expressive and receptive language skills so his ability with the computer has been used by the staff to work on these. He is encouraged to demonstrate and explain what he is doing and has now reached the stage of accepting that before he can use a different programme he has to talk through what he has done so far. He is becoming much more articulate and confident in his speech.

Another way of helping children who have problems in talking is to get them to explain the rules of simple games to the staff, or to another child or to the group and then to lead the whole group through the game. They usually need adult support to begin with but this is gradually withdrawn as they become more confident.

Some children continue to be reluctant to engage in conversation for a long time. A boy of seven would never chat however informal the situation and, unlike the other children, never sought out an adult to talk to. But he frequently looked at himself in the full-length wall mirror, often talking to himself in a range of voices. He sometimes dressed up and spoke to himself in role which gave the adults information about and insight into his feelings and preoccupations and opened up the possibility of being able eventually to join in his conversations.

An educational psychologist (Jaffey, 1990), researching nurture groups in Enfield, found that the children had opportunities to experience sustained conversations in the group and therefore both expected to be attended to and were more attentive themselves than in their normal classroom settings. She found that a qualitatively different verbal environment was generated in the nurture group, and concluded that the set-up in the groups is such as to enable the development of language to be given a high priority which had important implications for pupils' self-esteem, confidence and motivation.

Play

Play, it has been said, is children's work, and the ability to play vigorously comes naturally to the human young as it does to the young of the rest of the animal kingdom. Through play, young children develop physical skills. When they climb and run and skip, they are developing control over their movements; their physical confidence is growing and they are internalizing knowledge about themselves, how much space they occupy, and how to avoid other people's space. Through play with others – adults in the early stages and later other children of their own age – they are learning all sorts of relationship skills: how to share, how to take turns, when it is safe to assert oneself and when not. In short, through healthy, normal play children internalize an idea of themselves as capable beings, learn to organize themselves, and build up a repertoire of possible responses to different situations, all important skills for success in school

What children need for play is some suitable material, and the interest of a more experienced person to stimulate them. They then need safe space to play, which at first needs to be where adults can intervene immediately to protect them. As they become more competent, they move away a little at a time until they are taking considerable responsibility for their own safe management. It is part of adequate parenting to keep one's children safe while encouraging them stage by stage to greater independence.

Children may lack normal play opportunities for many reasons. There may be an unduly repressive atmosphere because parents are obsessively houseproud, or because neighbours are hostile. Less obviously, there may be serious emotional barriers to play. If parents are violent, or erratic in their response, a child may be too intimidated or depressed to play freely. If the child feels rejected, insecure, uncertain, play that explores the wider environment, that is not repetitive and familiar, may be too threatening. Some parents have no understanding of a child's need for emotional and physical space in which to play, try to impose inappropriate conditions and are angry when the child does not respond.

Poor housing conditions are one of the causes of family stress; there may physically not be any safe space to play, perhaps because the home is a high-rise flat, or bed and breakfast accommodation. Playing constructively is not an innate facility: it is something that has to be learnt. Children coming into school from such conditions need help in acquiring the skills, which has not always been understood in school. As the head teacher of an Inner London junior school said:

> There were terrible '60s tower blocks around us which produced children either in a vegetative state or extremely violent. They also helped to produce families, particularly one-parent families, where isolation had diminished the parents' ability to lead any sort of normal life. At one of the nearby infant schools, the school had a shed full of large toys that they kept locked up; the children were never allowed to use them. I was told that they had not learnt to share and they fought, so they could not have them till they learned. Now you can imagine this child from the 19th floor of a tower block; he had never seen a scooter in his life, so he grabbed it and he scooted on it and if somebody tried to take it away from him, he hit them. So they were not allowed to have them. If you devise in your mind the worst possible way to run a school for four to seven-year-olds it was there. The toys were in the shed: the children played round the shed: they could see them, the things they wanted to have. There was no understanding of why children could not play, that they had not had the opportunity to learn.

Nurture group children commonly reveal a lack of adequate experience of play. It shows in their lack of enterprise, of confidence, of physical skills, of body awareness; sometimes they seem almost not to know who they are or where their body starts and finishes. It is important therefore for nurture group rooms to be furnished and equipped in a way that encourages the sort of play that occurs in normal homes. By observing the children at play, the adults can judge the child's level of understanding and how best to intervene.

Many children in groups start to play early baby games, the 'peek a boo' game that most children delight in and grow out of in their first two years. Children of six or seven respond with baby delight to 'incy-wincy spider' or 'this little piggy' games, where their fingers and toes are counted; games and stories which have a repetitive element of 'what happened next' are popular: in short all the games and rituals by which babies and toddlers learn about themselves and about how the world works are still needed by nurture group children.

Mirrors

It is usual for nurture group rooms to have full-length mirrors to help children to a greater self-awareness than most of them possess. The children use them in revealing ways. A teacher described a boy of eight, big for his age and notorious in the playground for frequently knocking over smaller children, apparently oblivious of their presence. One day, he was seen with the dressing-up box, standing in front of the mirror, putting a hat on his head, and clearly not being sure the reflection was of him; lifting the hat off and putting it back on again, looking around to check that no other boy like him was there. He seemed to be asking, 'Is that me? Yes, it must be because I've just put the hat on.'

Contrast this with William, aged eight months, a well-loved child in a nurturing home, in his grandmother's arms in front of the big bathroom mirror. He looks at her in the mirror and then in the flesh, at first with surprise and then with pleasure. Then he looks at himself. Grandmother talks to his image, he laughs at her. His mother in the background joins in, calls his name and waves to his image. He waves back with delight, to the real mother and to the image; then the game spreads to his sister in the bath. By the end of that, there is no doubt that William knows more about himself, as the result of a normal family experience that is denied to some children.

Play as therapy

In psychotherapy with children, play is used to help them express what they cannot or dare not put into words. Through play they may relive traumatic events in their past and having thus been enabled to express their fears and accept reassurance, they then move on and make progress. Work with David in a play group in a child guidance centre will demonstrate the function of play in the treatment of emotionally disturbed children.

He was nearly six and was in dire distress in school. He was sad and preoccupied, did little work, hardly responded to his teacher, and was apparently afraid of the other children; very like many children admitted to nurture groups. He chose to spend much of his time alone in a corner. When he took to tearing up books and then to tearing up other children's clothes in the cloakroom, the school referred him for urgent child guidance help. Unable or unwilling to talk about his feelings, he was taken into a small play group.

At first he played silently with the sand and the cars in a repetitive way, only after some sessions allowing the therapist to join in his play but not making any verbal or eye contact. Then he took to looking at himself in the square mirror, pretending that he was appearing on television, singing jingles and having a conversation with himself. Eventually, the therapist was allowed into the conversations, which had to be conducted with David talking in the third person to the therapist: 'David is singing a song.'

The therapist responded and for the first time dialogue occurred, even if not in the first person, and although only about which pop star David was being. Any attempt to talk about real things made him retreat into silence. After a few sessions of this rather artificial communication, David suddenly grabbed the large pram in the playroom, mimed running a bath, got into the pram and imitated or actually experienced a massive tantrum, shouting and screaming, then taking on the role of an adult, shouting and threatening in gibberish.

The therapist knew from David's mother that she had been admitted to hospital suddenly, in an extremely depressed state, when David was three. Her husband was foreign-born and his family, whom David hardly knew and to whom he went as an emergency, spoke only limited English. His mother knew that David had been unhappy with them and he had been difficult to manage at home ever since, withdrawn and anxious, unwilling to let her out of his sight. She never understood what had gone on; David either would not or could not tell her anything about it. In the play group, it seemed that David had developed enough trust in the therapist to be able to act out his upset.

Eventually, after the bath incident, he slowly began to talk to the therapist in a manner appropriate to an intelligent six-year-old, about how frightened he had been by all that had happened to him. With adult acceptance and reassurance he rapidly became less anxious. He also began to be able to talk about his feelings at home with his loving and insightful mother and his behaviour and work at school improved remarkably. It may be assumed that he had thought of all sorts of explanations of what had happened to him which had been too frightening for him to articulate and which had influenced his view of himself and of the outside world.

Therapy through play raises to a professional level what happens quite normally in adequate families. Children who have been frightened will often play out whatever it is that has upset them. They may use their dolls to express anger or fear, and this is something which ordinary parents understand and allow. Many of the children who come to nurture groups have been exposed to experiences that they have found shocking, and which have made it difficult to trust adults. The opportunity in a group to build up trust in adults and to have safe space and time to play often lead to play which is clearly expressing something of great importance to the child. While it is stressed that nurture group staff are not psychotherapists, as they develop confidence in their skills they can allow and encourage such play, and if the staff need it, they have available the support of their educational psychologist.

Children may quite spontaneously get through some block to progress that adults can only vaguely suspect. As one of the nurture group teachers wrote:

> Children, once settled, often use the play material in the group and the presence of trusted adults to work out some early trauma. Staff have enough time and develop the skills to let this happen, and they stand by as a safe and silent presence while the child works out something which is clearly important to them.

Because the staff are aware of their children's lack of normal experiences, they become quick to see how games can help a child. One little girl of five had been diagnosed as an elective mute and had never been heard to speak in school by the time she was admitted to the nurture group. The class had a favourite story, 'In the dark, dark wood', where the children join in with actions and which ends up with everybody shouting 'Ghosts' amid general hilarity. One day the class duvet was used to simulate going into the dark wood; all the children pulled it over their heads. Everybody shouted out the responses enthusiastically from under the duvet. The staff realized that the 'mute' child had been shouting as loudly as the rest, after which she spoke normally in the group as though there had never been a problem.

A boy of six was admitted to a nurture group. He was one of twins, very much smaller than his brother who was coping in the normal class, and looked wizened as though he had failed to thrive. He was inconsequential, flitted from task to task and chattered incessantly. One day, he climbed into the big dog basket in the corner of the room, pulling the mattress on top of him. If the staff went near him he screamed and shouted, kicking his legs violently. Left to himself he lay in the basket apparently asleep. After doing this for quite a while each day he then took to sitting up in the basket. This went on for a few days, then he began to fill the basket with soft toys and sat among them, playing with them as though he were a baby. From that, he progressed to lying on the sofa and ordering a grown up to cover him with blanket. After a few days of that, what had seemed an intensely purposeful activity changed to a light-hearted game of going to bed on the sofa and asking to be covered up, a game in which he eventually lost interest. By then, he seemed much happier with himself, 'as though he had found out who he was' as his teacher said, and there was an all-round improvement. He made better relationships with the other children, and had better concentration so that his formal attainments improved.

Developing mathematical concepts

Mathematical concepts such as number, order, size, sequence, length, area, shape, volume, time and speed are in the beginning based on language concepts and, like them, in a nurturing home acquired as the child is ready for that stage of knowledge. Thus William, at 21 months, 'counts' unreliably if enthusiastically, 'one, three, four seven, nine, ten, coming!' as he plays hide and seek in the park with his family. Later, his grandmother plays the age-old game of counting his eyes, his ears, his lips and his nose. Then asked how many eyes he has got he says, 'two'; how many ears? 'two'; how many noses? 'two'. His grandmother repeats the ritual, two eyes, two ears, one nose. He triumphantly jabs grandmother's nose and says 'two'; laughter on both sides.

This becomes a family game with big sister Sally, nearly four, helping him. She then starts to count her fingers, five on one hand, five on the other.

How many altogether? William helps with imprecise enthusiasm. She shouts, 'How can I ever get to ten if you keep interrupting?' and the game ends. Slowly, and because it is enjoyable, William is learning the important facts, that numbers are not just words in a certain sequence but refer to specific quantities; he is acquiring the concept of conservation. As two-year-olds play with their puzzles they are absorbing all sorts of knowledge about shapes, and that shapes have names; as they pile up their blocks, about height and number; as they toss balloons they are learning about mass. For all this they need an interested and informed partner in their play.

Nurture group staff again and again comment on how the group children move through life uncomprehendingly, with little sense of correct sequences and, of course, a lack of basic concepts which are relevant both to literacy and numeracy. One teacher wrote:

> Many of the children seem to have no pattern of time. Days of the week, months, seasons, are meaningless concepts, so we have to talk about time a lot. During one such session, Darren, aged seven, asked, ' Does night always come after day, every time?'

A junior school head teacher reported:

> They would reach us at age seven and I did not believe it at first until I sat with them and listened to them, they did not know that Monday was followed by Tuesday, Tuesday by Wednesday and so on, and the Friday was always followed by THE WEEKEND. They still did not know that there were five school days and then the weekend, and then holidays. After seven years their life was still to them so unstructured that there was not a pattern called THE WEEK. So it is no wonder they did not know that 7 followed 6 and preceded 8, and they didn't. A great many of them did not know that they had five fingers. The group teacher taught me this: I did not believe her until I saw it. I sat in a session where she was playing a finger game. There were two seven-year-olds who did not know there were five of those on one hand and five on the other. Watching one of these boys who was the aggressive bully of the playground, saying 'Oohh' in delighted discovery, was terribly sad. It made you realize that there were other huge limits to their self-knowledge. And if they don't know about themselves, how are they going to know about other people?

Children who come into school without the experience of matching, and counting to find the number of objects in a set, will be handicapped in acquiring basic mathematical concepts, unless they are helped appropriately. Counting, and the four operations of addition, subtraction, division and multiplication, are usually learnt in stages, each one needing to be understood before the next one can be grasped.

Nurture group staff take every opportunity that arises in the group routines to develop awareness of mathematical concepts. Some of the staff of the ILEA nurture groups in the 1980s devised numerous strategies and projects with the help of Edith Biggs, HMI with a special responsibility for mathematics, who found the relaxed atmosphere and positive attitude to learning in the groups most impressive. With her help, the staff raised to a more complex level the mathematical concepts they were already teaching, always starting by involving the children in ways that started from their current level of interest.

When teachers begin to work with the four operations, they find that the one which lends itself most easily to the practical approach is division, where problem situations can be solved by the children themselves. Halving is often the first experience of division and in one group the children began halving a variety of objects and materials.

'Share the ribbon fairly,' the teacher urged them; then she asked them what this meant.

Philip said, 'Make two equal halves.'

The teacher than gave each of the children a length of ribbon and some scissors. Philip began by trying to find the middle of the ribbon by eye, marked his chosen point in pencil, and cut it. Jane put the two ends of the ribbon together, folded it and cut along the fold. Then they discussed the merits of the two methods. At 'breakfast' one child can be in charge of the packet of biscuits, giving each person two each. How many biscuits are needed for that? Then comes the question of the number left over. Are there enough for everyone to have another biscuit? If not what is a fair thing to do?

Modelling with plasticine, the children are shown how to halve it by weighing out each lump on the classroom scales. When they have made each lump into an animal, they are asked which is the heavier and they check with the scales, so learning about conservation of weight. They are helped to notice how the water level goes up as the doll goes into the bath; this leads to getting them to make judgements about how much water should be put into containers if the water is not to overflow when objects are added, and so ideas of volume and capacity are introduced.

The children had to decide which of two tablecloths they would use for breakfast, one which covered the whole table, or one which left the edges bare. Later, they looked for a table with a smaller top that could be covered completely, which led to discussion of area. One group changed to having transparent tumblers for their morning drink so that they could estimate quantity better when they were pouring out. When they are playing with the clothes from the dressing-up box, they use ideas of fit: too small, too long, too tight; and of time and growth: how long will it be before this coat will fit? Who is the tallest in the group?

One group of five-year-olds began to move from mathematical to scientific concepts such as mass, speed and friction when their teacher noticed how fascinated some of the children were by the speed with which different toy vehicles went down the ramps they had constructed in the classroom. Their teacher wrote:

> We started with body awareness. It was summertime, so we went to the park, where there is a good slope, taking with us on different occasions such things as wheeled toys, tin trays, a sheet of polythene and dressing-up clothes. We started by all of us rolling down the slope, and we marked with a tent peg the point each of us reached. When we had had a lot of fun rolling down, we measured the distance we had rolled ... We used the children's feet, walking heel to toe and counting. We noted the effect of different body weights on the distance rolled, and then tried rolling down the slope in different clothing to see if that made a difference, and we compared being pushed with a free roll. We then rolled down the slope on different surfaces, on grass, on a blanket, on a large piece of polythene.
>
> The children enjoyed these total body activities. All took part with interest and enthusiasm, and the most unsettled child in the group threw himself onto the hill, eager to see how far he could roll, and was genuinely interested to find out that when he tucked his shirt in he went faster, and that the position of his hands determined the extent to which he skewed off course ... Back in the classroom, we set up ramps and varied the gradient of the slope to see how far cars would travel up the other side. Then we added two other dimensions: different sizes of vehicles and different textured material on the gradients – velvet, fur fabric, silk, wool. Everybody was fascinated and amazed. We provided a running commentary on these experiments, introducing and drawing from the children the notions of heaviness, lightness, and the effects of textures and of gradients.
>
> All the children came to the group with extremely limited concentration, unable to follow through a theme. Most of them had been in the group for two terms and were more organized and purposeful, but the sessions were nevertheless carefully controlled and structured with stress on queueing up, taking turns and going one at a time and everything was taken slowly. They took part with enthusiasm, and over this period there was a surprising development of their motor coordination and body awareness; they seemed to grasp the concepts underlying these experiments intuitively, and understood them.

Flexible adult response to children's needs

What is obvious in talking to teachers and assistants in nurture groups is how confident they feel in taking initiatives, as they would when presented with a problem by their own child. Because it is recognized that age-appropriate teaching strategies have not worked with these children, the adults have the freedom and authority to reassess and change. Predictability and routine are an important part of the ethos, as has been stressed, but rituals are not inconsistent with a rapid change in response when it is indicated.

In Enfield, cookery time for all the children at once was not working out, because of the attention each child needed; so the class agreed to have a rota. Two children did the cooking each time and everybody ate the buns. Some children enjoyed checking their place on the rota.

Although usually nurture group children join their base class in the playground, one child having difficulty in managing his behaviour outside agrees to help the staff in clearing up from 'breakfast'. A boy is quite unable to manage being with other children, rapidly disrupting the whole class every morning; so instead of going to his base class, his mother brought him direct to the group room where he worked calmly so that he had a better start to the day.

Teachers can also do things which would simply not be possible in a mainstream class. A child beginning to assert himself threatens, when frustrated, to run away. The adult says, as many a mother has said, 'Well, I shall be very sorry to lose you, but if that's what you want, I can't stop you.' The child then walks out and round the playground, with the teacher following at a distance, out of his sight. Eventually he returns, forgives the adults and settles down. A girl threatened again and again to run away. Finally the teacher got her school bag and, asking her kindly what she wanted put in it, packed it and started to take her towards the school gate. Halfway there, the girl decided to stay in the group, came back and her threats were not repeated. Both children have experienced choice and control in a safe setting.

A teacher is concerned about a new child, a boy of eight, who is thought perhaps to be autistic and who markedly either avoids eye contact or appears to look through people. On the school bus, he looks at her unseeingly. She looks back and rolls her eyes horribly. 'We looked at each other in stony silence. I rolled my eyes again, and again. Suddenly he copied me: I did it again and he copied. We both laughed, and from then on he began to relate more normally.'

One little boy had frequent screaming, stamping tantrums. His teacher stood in front of him and, with no anger, also screamed and stamped and generally simulated a tantrum. The boy stopped in surprise and watched with interest. His tantrums declined rapidly in number and intensity after that.

Effective intervention and school morale

In Enfield, it is emphasized again and again that LEA policy is for nurture groups to be a central feature of the life of the school. When nurture groups are a successful, integral part of the school their teachers feel valued and supported. They cooperate with the mainstream class teacher to give the child an explicit and supportive framework; the class teacher learns from the insights which the group teacher has gained from her privileged position and their work reinforces each other's. This was also the experience in the ILEA groups, as a junior head teacher said:

> The whole core of the nurture group is that the benefit to the child is doubled because of all the good feedback. The quickest way to set up a sin bin is to try to run a nurture group without the genuine support of most of the teachers and the head. Then, everybody will see it as a dumping ground for their problems and they will be resentful if their problem does not get dumped. For a nurture group teacher battling alone against all that and unable to share their experience with the other teachers, it would not work. Nor would it work for the child. When the group is running properly, if the child has done well there he comes out and goes into his base classroom, and the child and the teacher are much better set up to succeed together for the rest of the time.

> The class teacher has had a break and the child comes back with positive accounts of what he has been doing. There is also that inter-supporting structure, the class teacher being able to say to the group teacher, 'He really tried hard at swimming yesterday, and I was very pleased with him. He behaved himself, he didn't run like last week. I thought he did very well.' The group teacher is then able to follow that up as well, in front of the child and in front of the other children, building the child's confidence and self-esteem. Very occasionally the contact is used to set boundaries. 'I'm terribly disappointed. You know how good at maths he was last week, well this week he behaved in such a silly way. He threw his pencil on the floor.' 'Oh you didn't! That was really bad. And we had already talked about that.' This is important. They are all on the side of the child, praising achievements and setting standards.

> This means that all the teachers in the school are encouraged to look at children as individuals and speculate on what they are really making of their education and what strategies can be tried to help them to do better. Instead of the stereotypical, somewhat dismissive judgemental remarks we had all grown up with – 'nice little girl, no trouble, doesn't read very well' – after the introduction of the nurture group they would use different words, would turn things round very sharply. 'Lucy isn't reading because ... I haven't enough time to give her.'

> Initially, teachers found it hard to identify anything but the aggressive, outgoing children. We got over that by the sharpening of the professional observation of all the staff; the fact that they were beginning to look at their child not as a success or a failure, not as a good child or a bad child, but why can't this child . . . ? What does this child . . . ? I wonder why this child

is no trouble . . . ? It took a couple of years for that question to come up. They were so used to categorizing children as 'trouble' or 'no trouble' that the question of whether that child was benefiting at all from school was ignored. One of our great successes, I felt, as a staff was identifying one or two children in every class, usually little girls, who were no trouble, who were gaining nothing at all from school. They were probably living in fear. They didn't tear the books up. Teachers just wrote them off as not academic, 'a nice little girl but not very bright'. Quite often they could have been very clever. One wonders about the dozens of wasted school lives.

Nurture groups began to build up enormous confidence in teachers: they knew they could effect change in children. Anyone with eyes to see and prepared to listen must have found going into schools where nurture theory was being discussed that teachers were more articulate and confident and with a better vocabulary for talking about children positively and with some degree of careful thought about what they were going to say.

The head teacher of an ILEA infant school wrote:

Before the setting up of the nurture group (in the late 1970s) teachers felt a lack of expertise to meet the needs of disruptive or withdrawn children. The withdrawn were not given the attention that teachers knew they needed. The disruptive were seen solely as a problem, to be removed from the class and sent to the head teacher when too difficult for the class teacher to manage, a technique which often fed the child's need for attention and so solved nothing. Referral to the educational psychologist got responses only after long delays, and the advice then given, while helpful, required more resources than the school could provide. Parents, asked to school to discuss their child's behaviour, were often defensive, feeling guilty, resentful, blaming or angry: feelings which increased in intensity as the child's behaviour failed to improve.

As the nurture group progressed, the staff as a whole became more aware of how children develop, which helped curriculum development as a whole. The management of the classes became easier in the mornings, which was when the group was in action, as there were fewer disruptions. The class teachers, through discussion with the nurture teacher, felt supported in meeting the needs of the nurture group child. The teachers' attitudes changed from seeing the whole child as a problem to seeing his behaviour in terms of his developmental stage. When the nurture group child rejoined his or her class in the afternoon, the teacher was more likely to behave more positively towards them. Because of the beneficial experiences in the nurture group, the child would be likely to be less demanding of attention.

Many parents, in discussing their child with the nurture group teacher, became more positive towards him or her. They began to identify success in their child's work and behaviour and somehow seemed to view their child as more 'worthwhile'.

It is sad to note that the nurture group described here was closed in 1993. The introduction of LMS (Local Management of Schools) meant that there was no extra funding available for the group. The new LEA was not inclined to fund such a group separately as they were, as a matter of policy, committed to children having their special needs met totally within the mainstream class. They were not sympathetic to any form of withdrawal, even though a special needs inspector shortly before its closure praised the work going on in the group. The head teacher and one of her colleagues wrote about the change:

> The nurture group had catered for 10 to 12 children, who were collected from their classrooms first thing, spent the morning working with the nurture group teacher and helper and returned to their own classrooms for the afternoon session with the nurture group team providing support and working alongside their teachers. The class teachers valued having the morning without the 'nurture' children. It gave them the opportunity to teach their class without a disproportionate amount of time going to one or two children. They knew the nurture group children were being given skills and strategies that meant the afternoons went better too.
>
> The loss of the nurture group is seen as a great blow for everyone. Demanding children now take up more of the class teacher's time at the expense of other children in the class. Withdrawn children who formerly would also have been in the nurture group suffer from the lack of one-to-one time and of a small group in which to learn how to cope. Intervention following the Code of Practice is less effective as it cannot provide the same concentration of resources to establish strategies and skills. Achieving apparently simple goals, such as making eye contact or sitting on the carpet with the class, becomes more difficult in a class of 30 without the support the nurture group provided in the optimal setting. Classes appear to staff to be less purposeful and regrets are constantly expressed as to the nurture group's going.
>
> The nurture group helper was retained and became a special needs assistant working with identified children in Years 1 and 2 who get, on average, about two hours a week. For children who need nurture input, this is a drop in the ocean. It is also so inefficient of resources and time. Moving from classroom to classroom with equipment scattered around in different places and trying to function in a busy classroom when what is needed is no distraction makes the assistant's task all the more difficult. There is a

reading recovery programme in the school which in some ways caters for the children who previously would have been in the nurture group. In a similar way, through intense adult involvement, it teaches skills, builds up self-confidence and leads to better behaviour, but it caters for no more than six children a year compared to the 10 or 12 of the nurture group.

It is also interesting to note that the school moves to statementing much more now. In effect, the nurture group was covering Stages 2 and 3 of the Code of Practice thoroughly and effectively. Children were achieving and feeling good about themselves and there was less need to statement. Early intervention paid off. It is also felt that there has been a loss in the areas of behaviour and ethos. The group encouraged the dissemination of strategies relevant to the whole class and school. It led to more positive attitudes to special needs children among staff and pupils. There seem to be more negative discussions now in the staff room. There is a sense that such children are now the class teacher's responsibility entirely and they do feel more harassed. It is also of note that the school has had a permanent exclusion for the first time within anyone's memory.

It will be clear from this account that a school's morale has been damaged and it cannot be emphasized too much that good school morale is essential if children are to be adequately helped in mainstream school. The aim of the Code of Practice is to stop as far as humanly possible the waste of children's educational chances, but it will not work if teachers feel that its aims are unrealistic. There is no point in identifying children as needing special help if that help cannot then be given, whether because of resources or because of an LEA policy which may seem to be based on doctrine rather than on a realistic awareness of children's needs.

OFSTED reports

One of the Enfield schools with a nurture group from which much of the material in this chapter was drawn was inspected by the Office for Standards in Education; the brief extracts from their report, below, will give some idea of the quality of the school's work.

[The school] serves an area of predominantly local authority housing in the London Borough of Enfield. Unemployment in the immediate area is above the national average and 38% of pupils are eligible for free school meals. There are 272 pupils on roll and a 60 place nursery which the majority of pupils attend before their reception year.

The pupil intake represents a wide range of ability and initial assessments indicate that a number of children have limited social and literacy skills on starting school. Across the school, 99 pupils are identified as having special educational needs and the school has a ten place nurture group. (1.2)

[The] nurture group for pupils with particular emotional needs provides excellent support and enables the children to cope with, and adjust to, normal school life. It is run by competent and professional staff and is very effective in providing a secure learning environment. Staff make careful and thorough assessments of the pupils and demonstrate a perceptive understanding of their needs. A good range of activities is provided which pupils enjoy and through which they can make sound progress. (7.4.3)

[The school] makes a marked contribution to pupils' learning and achievement. It is a supportive and secure community where all pupils are known, valued and cared for by conscientious and committed staff. Standards of achievement in the Nursery and for the youngest pupils are consistently good and the children's social development is particularly good. At Key Stage 1 the majority of pupils achieve national expectations and pupil achievement is sound to good in relation to their abilities. (2.1.1)

Overall, pupil behaviour is good and the school has well established routines which result in a secure and orderly learning environment. The school's caring ethos effectively supports pupils' learning and achievement. (2.1.7)

The head teacher and her deputy, interviewed, are in no doubt that the presence and the work of the nurture group played a central part throughout the school in the achievement of these high standards.

Chapter 5

Preventing Educational Failure

Marion Bennathan

Recent changes in legislation, notably the 1988 Education Act, had the laudable aim of improving access for all children to good quality education and were not intended to make it even more difficult for disadvantaged children to succeed. That this, as was discussed earlier, appears to have been the result, suggests a lack of understanding of the realities of life in school for many such children. It therefore seems appropriate to look briefly at some of the ideas and assumptions which have, over the last generation, influenced thinking and policy about children and their education, and why they fail or why they succeed.

Understanding such children is important for policy-makers. It is equally important for teachers since it is they who have to deliver the education service and their perception of deviant behaviour or poor progress and its causes will significantly influence their reaction to their pupils. A great many teachers concerned to make the Code of Practice work for children whose special educational needs come from social disadvantage are urgently seeking effective approaches; teachers who know of the work of the nurture groups find that their principles explain educational failure convincingly and that their methods work. But the search for ways of preventing educational failure is not new and it is important to understand how the nurture group way of thinking fits into the wider framework.

IQ as an explanation of educational failure

The idea of the intelligence quotient, the IQ, as a scientific and accurate measure of human intellectual potential held great sway over the education system from the 1930s. It helped to shape the 1944 Education Act which divided children into groups capable or not of academic education, with group tests of intelligence forming a considerable part of the selection procedures at the age of 11. Its centrality to thinking about educational progress continued through the next three decades. Children, it was broadly assumed, did well educationally because they were of good intelligence, and failed because they were born with low ability. This equation of ability and attainment has had disastrous consequences for some children. One example, from the writer's personal experience, will make the point:

A young head teacher, taking over a large junior school in an area of considerable social deprivation, found his pupils coming up from the infant school already sorted by the infant school head into an A class, a B class and C class. The infant head teacher was a lady of great authority who had been in post for 30 years and who had been close friends with the former head of the junior school. The practice had gone on for many years, and it took some time for the new head teacher to find out on what principles the children were segregated. It seemed partly that the infant head teacher knew the families, and did not expect some children to do well; 'That sort of child' was the phrase used.

Eventually it seemed that the criterion used was the level of reading the children had reached. Those able to read at the average level for their age went into the A class; those who were somewhat retarded in reading went into the B class where some extra help was available; those who were illiterate went into the C class and were given no extra help in reading on the grounds that they were too dull to profit by it. The educational psychologist, as appalled as the new head teacher, spent some days in the school, examined the reading levels of each class and confirmed that the classes were indeed ranked in order of reading attainment. She then tested all the children on a group intelligence test, one which measured verbal understanding, and was presented pictorially.

There was very little difference in the average scores of the three classes, and very few children in class C with scores low enough to suggest that poor ability was the cause of their reading difficulties. The results of the survey were presented to the staff group who were quite astonished; they had assumed that Class C were hardly above the 'educationally subnormal' level and certainly extremely limited in their verbal skills. The staff then began to reflect on the children in Class C; that many of them were members of large and problem-laden families, well known in the district and in the school. The new head teacher had no difficulty then in changing the school's structure and two years later literacy and attainments had improved greatly.

Some of the reliance of educationalists on over-simple ideas of inherited ability was due to the great authority of Cyril Burt, the first educational psychologist to be appointed by a local authority. His widely publicized fall from grace, well documented by Hearnshaw (1979), when the data on which he had based his work was alleged to be fraudulent, was one of the many factors which lessened the reliance on IQ testing. It is a gross oversimplification to say that Burt, or other educational psychologists at the time, simply tested children's intelligence (a practice disrespectfully called 'Binet-bashing' by a later generation of psychologists), and, if they scored low, automatically categorized them as needing special education.

Many children judged by their teachers on the basis of the work they produced in class as needing to be educated elsewhere showed themselves able to function at an average level or better in an individual test. The gap between the IQ scored and the level of work achieved in class often led to the conclusion that the causes of failure had to be sought elsewhere than in the child's innate ability. This in turn might lead to changes either in school or at home, much to the child's advantage. On the whole, however, it is probably true to say that if a child scored a low enough IQ the assumption was that this was proof of low innate ability and a special school would be recommended.

By the 1960s those of us who were training and working as educational psychologists were coming to see that the emphasis on IQs was beginning to limit rather than help our understanding of why some children were failing educationally. This is not to say that all children were being thought of as born with equal intellectual potential, but the contribution of early experience, early learning and present social circumstances to the level a child reached in a test was becoming widely recognized.

The acknowledgement of the unreliability of the assessed IQ as the main indicator of educational need was also hastened by the large numbers of children from ethnic minorities coming into schools. It was claimed that tests measured innate ability, but it was coming to be recognized that they were in fact much more culture-specific than had previously been thought; differences in language, in background information, in attitudes to adults, all had their effect. There was also a great increase in political awareness of the class-related sources of educational inequality. By 1969, Vernon, a leading expert on intelligence and its assessment, was writing, 'Psychological theories of intelligence have altered very drastically since the 1920s, and this has led to a fresh interpretation of individual, social class and ethnic differences.'

We cannot do more here than acknowledge the emergence and the importance of these concerns. The brilliant book by Gould (1981) *The Mismeasurement of Man*, demonstrates convincingly the many errors in thinking and in research method which led American psychologists in the 1920s and '30s to the conclusion that by and large 'intelligence' was innate and was closely correlated with social class and wealth, Americans of white Anglo-Saxon stock coming highest. It is somewhat depressing to see the same over-simple views of 'innate' ability once again given publicity today by Herrnstein and Murray (1994) whose book on intelligence and class structure suggests a very close correlation between social competence and innate ability, with the worrying implication that if these things are ordained by nature, there is little point in measures to improve the position of the disadvantaged. Perhaps Charles Darwin is a better guide to the nature of humanity. He wrote, in *The Voyage of the Beagle*, 'if the misery of our poor be caused not by the laws of nature but by our institutions, great is our sin.'

Certainly, working with children who are failing educationally one becomes aware of a great loss of potential; of unmotivated, disaffected children whose lives are going to be much less enjoyable and worthwhile than they might have been if they had become positively engaged in the educational process. Whatever their IQ scores, they function at a low level and they urgently need help. One example will make the point:

> Tommy was referred to the psychologist at the age of nine because he was making no progress in the good junior school he attended. He was living in a family group home, with kindly and long-established staff, having been taken into the care of the local authority as a small boy after much work to help his middle-aged and mentally confused mother to look after him adequately had failed. Every week he spent Saturday afternoon waiting at the window of the home for his mother to visit. Sometimes she came, but more often and without explanation failed to appear. When seen at school, Tommy enjoyed the psychologist's attention and worked amiably on the test material, scoring an IQ of 91. He was, however, barely able to read and seemed resigned to his state. Asked if he thought of himself as average, or clever, or not very clever, he said flatly and seriously, 'I am crap'. It was not possible to motivate him, or his teacher with a class of 35, to do enough to get his reading going and it seemed best to put him in the excellent nearby school for the 'educationally subnormal' and hope that, with the extra attention there, he would improve enough to be moved back to a normal school, which he never did.

The interest in social deprivation

The 1960s and '70s saw a growing interest in the connection between social conditions and educational success. The work which above all focused attention on the connection between social conditions and educational attainment was the celebrated National Child Development Study, initiated by Neville Butler, Mia Kellmer Pringle, Ronald Davie and colleagues, and still ongoing. This follows the development – physical, social, educational – of virtually all the children born in one week in March 1958 and has resulted in many influential publications. In *From Birth to Seven* (Davie *et al.*, 1972) it was pointed out that by the age of seven there were 'some interesting and disturbing facts about social class differences and their effect on children's development'. The study began to map out precisely the correlation between educational attainment and such factors as parental income, educational status, housing standards, and size of family.

The study has made an important contribution to our understanding of children's development and of the effectiveness of public services. But alerting the educational world to these facts did not in itself suggest ways in which teachers in the classroom could overcome the effects of social disadvantage. Indeed, teachers could and did interpret its message negatively. If social conditions are so important, how can we have high expectations of children from poor and unsupportive homes? 'I am a teacher not a social worker' was a popular response to the research findings; the message received by many schools was over-simple. The researchers never claimed that there was more than a correlation between social conditions and educational attainments, not a precise causal connection. Poor homes are not necessarily bad homes: some parents can provide loving and stimulating care on a low income. To stereotype children because of their background can lead to disastrously low teacher expectations and hence poor progress. The interest in social deprivation which the study stimulated and documented did not in itself lead to better teaching strategies.

The influence of experts

Another growth area in the field of special education was in services for 'maladjusted' children, first officially recognized as having an educational disability in the 1944 Education Act. This was partly prompted by concern about the number of children awaiting placement as 'educationally subnormal' or 'maladjusted'. The Underwood Committee which reported in 1955 recommended an increase in the number of educational psychologists and child guidance clinics, and the expansion of the number of training courses for teachers of the 'maladjusted'.

The report was not set up to consider the greater part that mainstream schools could play in the better management of such children nor the question of whether some of the children's difficulties were the result of what happened to them in school. It is not to devalue the work of the professional groups who grew in number as a result of the report to say that, on the whole, their function was not seen as something to be shared with schools in a sense that really affected the ethos of the whole school. Their work was often seen as medically based and mysterious.

A London head teacher, describing her search for help for the large numbers of her pupils who were not coping with mainstream education, gives a somewhat acid description of her local child guidance clinic which sadly, although there were areas of excellent practice, was not untypical of the relationship between services:

> As a new head I was learning the rules about child guidance clinics. Nobody told you what these things were, you had to find out by trial and error. It seemed to me that child guidance clinics hated schools and teachers, particularly heads and that you must not be included in the work; you had to disappear into the wallpaper. It was a sort of trick, where you convinced the parent that they desperately wanted to go there and if they wouldn't go any more inevitably it was your fault. Child guidance would phone up and say, 'They didn't come. What did you do?' It all seemed to me a sort of trick to keep you quiet about children who should not be in your school.

This head teacher would have found support for her views from Tizard who, in 1973, published a paper attacking the wasteful and ineffectual organization of child guidance services and their lack of impact on schools:

> Psychologists and sociologists have been incurious about the influence of the school in affecting behaviour. On the whole they have tended to accept the view...that variations among schools are not associated with variations in the prevalence of maladjusted behaviour... Very many children dislike school, are bored with school or are unhappy there. It is, however, rare for anyone to make a systematic study of why ordinary children find difficulties in adjusting to school... Contact (of educational psychologists) with schools was not great. .... The average teacher, indeed, doesn't get much direct help from any of the special services: contact with the school doctor is often fleeting or non-existent, remedial teachers often take children out of the class rather than help teachers in the class, educational advisers may visit only infrequently, and the psychiatrist and social worker not at all. In consequence, the average teacher lacks advice; and equally often lacks the skill to deal with particular problems.

The paper, needless to say, caused great upset in the child guidance movement and was unfair to services who were tackling the very issues Tizard identified in the plans they were required to produce in 1974 at the time of local government reorganization. Nevertheless it made valid points. Such services were not regarded as having a duty to change practice in schools, and for the most part did not do so. The best run services no doubt addressed the problem of joint work with children, their families and their teachers by staff from different professional backgrounds, and responsible to different employers, but very few approached the state of being easily accessible to all teachers and thereby able to influence whole schools.

The mystique of special schools

Another factor that stood in the way of mainstream teachers recognizing how many more children with difficulties could be kept in mainstream schools was their lack of first-hand knowledge of special schools. Many requests for special placement were made from a basis of ignorance, since it is not a part of normal teacher training to gain experience of special provision. Moreover, the very existence of special schools for the 'maladjusted' or the 'educationally subnormal' may suggest to the mainstream teacher that there were skills for teaching children in difficulties which they themselves did not possess, so that conscientious teachers were implicitly encouraged to ask for children in difficulties to be moved. Again, teaching is highly demanding work: the job is open-ended. It could always be done better if there were more time. It might be in the child's interests to move them to somewhere special where they would get more skilled help. Then, the extra attention needed by a child in difficulties has to be given at the expense of the rest of the class, so also for their sake the temptation is to arrange for the removal of that child.

As part of a course on children with learning difficulties[1] the students, all experienced teachers, spent some days in special schools. A standard reaction from mainstream teachers to a day in a school for children with moderate learning difficulties was one of shock: the realization that teachers there were only doing what they themselves did, if at a slower pace and with more individual attention and tolerance than is possible in a mainstream class. 'I could do all of that if I had the resources' was a frequent comment.

Of course some children have difficulties that are too great for them to be helped in mainstream class, so they need special placement of one kind or another, and special schools have been and are supportive and positive places for some children. But if policy, for the children's sake, as well as to make the best use of resources, is to help as many children as possible in mainstream, all teachers need to understand what they can do and what is beyond them, so a knowledge of what special schools do ought to be a part of every teacher's initial training.

The Warnock Report: a missed opportunity

The committee chaired by Mary Warnock reported in 1978, its main findings being made law in the 1981 Education Act. One of its central recommendations was the abolition of the categorizing of children. Instead of saying that a child was 'deaf' or 'maladjusted', the child's educational needs should be precisely assessed and a statement of the provision that would exactly meet them should be drawn up.

A great flurry of activity was provoked in the educational world in anticipation of the implementation of the 1981 Act, but this concentrated very considerably on the rival merits of 'segregated' and 'integrated' provision, and on the procedural changes required by the Act. There was not a great deal of discussion of what underlay the abolition of categorizing, the important shift in thinking which comes from the growing understanding of the many processes which affect educational progress.

Many children were, in the past, put forward for special education not because they were suffering from an inborn condition which accounted for their failure in mainstream school but because they had not had the extra help they needed in mainstream, particularly at the early stages of their education. The child comes into school from a disadvantaged background, appears to be dull and is accepted as such, as in the Bristol junior school described above. The child's self-esteem suffers; she or he accepts what is seen as the school's judgement and becomes apathetic and perhaps disaffected.

The Warnock Report recognized this and recommended that all schools should have early assessment and monitoring procedures. Some educational psychology services[2] took the opportunity of the 1981 Act to help schools to review practice in the light of the recommendations of the report, but changing the attitude of all teachers to children who are failing is a complex task. Overall the needs of the 18 per cent of children in mainstream suggested by the Warnock Report as requiring some extra help were, as was discussed earlier, not much better met after Warnock than before. The tighter system of identification and monitoring in all schools brought about by the 1993 Code of Practice will perhaps have more success. Its chances will be greater if teachers really believe that they can effect significant change for their disadvantaged pupils.

The child's point of view

There is a source of information about children and their progress which has not been much used, and this is the children themselves. Their perception of their situation is crucial if we are to plan effective help. It has not been customary in official educational policy to give much attention to what the pupil thinks. The 1989 Children Act, generally considered to embody the principles of good practice in work with children, takes as one of its central tenets the need for the child's voice to be heard. Children have a point of view and must be consulted about decisions which affect them. By contrast, consulting the pupil gets no mention in the 1988 Education Act. This is a surprising omission which, happily, has at last been made good and the right of children to be heard is now acknowledged in educational legislation. The Code of Practice sets out in detail the benefits that come from involving children in the assessment of and intervention in their special educational needs: 'Their support is crucial to the effective implementation of any individual education programme' (2.34–2.36).

Listening to children is becoming increasingly accepted as desirable in mainstream as in special education and interest is growing as can be seen, for example, in *Listening to Children in Education* (Bennathan, 1995), edited by Davie and Galloway, which demonstrates that 'listening to children is found to be both practical and effective'. While young children clearly do not have the ability to contribute to a discussion of their situation at a level of equality with adults, they express unease or disquiet in many ways, and their ability to formulate their worries develops quite early.

In *Listening to Children in Education* (Bennathan, 1995, pp. 102–3), the head teacher of an infant school tells how she consulted the children about the school assembly which was not working well. Small children could analyse what was going wrong – being kept waiting because other classes were late, children showing their work but talking about it inaudibly and for too long. Even five-year-olds could express their embarrassment about the head teacher being cross with the whole school in assembly; they felt it would be easier to put up with this in the smaller setting of their own classroom, a suggestion which was accepted.

The child's perception

Underlying the principle of consulting the child is the acknowledgement that it is children's perception of events and not objective reality which governs their reactions. From an early age, they have a view about events that affect them. They form a concept of themselves from the way they have been treated and through this they then assess what is happening to them. Thus, young children left in hospital unvisited by their parents might feel that they were bad, had done something wrong for which they were being abandoned for ever. They would then react to their parents on their return home with anger or extreme anxiety or mistrust, and thus set in train a process of maldevelopment unless the parents had the understanding and the resources to help the child through its difficulties. Children who are adopted often feel that it was some fault in them that made their birth parents give them away, and they may need reassurance that this was not so. Children whose parents divorce need to be helped not to feel responsible for the grown-ups' quarrels.

In short, children take a highly personal view of their lives which shapes their judgements and the fact that these may not be well based in reality does not make them any the less powerful. In the case of children with marked emotional and behavioural difficulties it is not primarily their reasoning abilities that are at fault so much as the base from which they start. Most behaviour, however outrageous and even self-destructive, makes sense if seen through the eyes of the behaver. Or as Voltaire wrote in 1764 in his *Philosophical Dictionary*, madness is a state in which the sufferer 'has erroneous perceptions and thereafter reasons correctly from them'.

All young children see the world from an egocentric standpoint. They lack the intellectual capacity and skills to view what happens to them in an objectively reasonable framework. With slow and painstaking teaching from parents and teachers they learn to consider events from a less self-centred perspective. Children with consistently bad early experiences are not necessarily 'mad', but they frequently have a negative view of adults which they bring to their relationship with their teachers, to whom they react adversely, perhaps by aggression, perhaps by withdrawal. This is a most important truth for teachers to understand if they are to respond as effectively as they might to children's behaviour. Many teachers go through their working lives assuming that it is some deficiency in them or in their teaching that causes some children to react negatively to them. Such an attitude wastes the teacher's energy and generates negative emotions which inhibit the search for better ways of managing difficult behaviour.

Children's feelings

This recognition that young children have strong feelings and that emotional understanding, or misunderstanding, precedes rational thought is of central importance. It is well recognized in paediatric practice that physical growth is influenced by emotional factors. There is, for example, the 'failure to thrive' syndrome (now recognized as *reactive attachment disorder*, and discussed later) where a baby fails to make normal developmental progress, fails to gain weight appropriately even though adequate food is provided (see, for example, Forfar and Arneil, *Textbook of Paediatrics*, 1992). Removed from the negative atmosphere of the home to a children's ward in hospital, the baby grows in responsiveness and in weight; returned home, development falters. In a similar vein, Baroness Lucy Faithfull, a renowned worker for children and one of the architects of the 1989 Children Act, writes of the effects on children's physical growth of being separated from their parents because of evacuation in the Second World War:

In Islington ... I was involved in a research study of the effect the war had on children. We visited the families where children had stayed with their parents and hadn't been to school, didn't have school milk and slept with their parents in the Underground and compared them with those who had gone to good billets in the country with good education and good food, but were parted from their families. The research showed that the children who had stayed with their families were taller and heavier and emotionally better than the children who were evacuated ... That research taught me how disastrous it is to separate children from their parents.[3]

Thus in many areas of work with children, the centrality of the child's feelings about their situation is accepted and a conscious effort is made to understand them and to reassure and support them through their misunderstandings. The sense of self and the ability to form trusting relationships which come from the quality of early experiences is as central to educational progress as it is to physical and social development and this recognition needs to be enshrined in educational policy and practice. It is interesting to speculate why educational practice and theorizing has traditionally paid such scant attention to children's feelings. Perhaps authoritative explanations, such as those of the primacy of innate ability, have delayed this recognition. If, for example, we are convinced that a child's ability is essentially fixed at birth, we will not challenge their functioning at a low level. But once the developmental input to educational progress is recognized, the way is open for vigorous in-school intervention. Two examples of such intervention, Instrumental Enrichment and High/Scope will now be considered.

Action in the classroom: 1. Instrumental Enrichment

Instrumental Enrichment is one of the projects for helping teachers to intervene early with disadvantaged children that have been considered promising enough to attract public funding. The movement was started in the 1960s by Reuven Feuerstein, a psychologist who trained with Piaget and started work with immigrant children in Israel in the late 1940s. Some of the children had been born to parents in the terrible conditions brought about by the Holocaust; others were from Jewish communities expelled from North African countries where they had passed their early lives in traditional, even primitive, circumstances, often with little formal education. They had been through the trauma of exile, and had come to a country with a highly organized and technologically advanced society.

In helping to develop resettlement programmes for these children, Feuerstein realized that their low scores on conventional testing procedures reflected their lack of learning rather than their lack of native ability. He devised a new test, the Learning Potential Assessment Device. The essence of this is that the child is set a task. If it is too difficult for them, they are then given help and observations are made about how well they use the help and how quickly they improve their performance. The next stage is that the child is given 'instruments' which are teaching programmes, carefully sequenced and largely perceptual and visual rather than verbal which, it is claimed, teach skills of forming concepts, of thinking, of reasoning, which then generalize to other areas of intellectual activity. He described his work in his book, published in 1969, *The Instrumental Enrichment Method: An Outline of Theory and Techniques.*

Feuerstein's ideas excited considerable interest in the educational world in the early 1980s, with press headlines such as, 'Intelligence can be taught'. The Schools Council, a government-funded body, financed the publicizing of the scheme. Training courses were set up and several education authorities in the UK invested in the training of teachers and in the rather expensive American material needed. Feuerstein himself is a charismatic figure, a brilliant lecturer, whose zeal for finding and developing ability in children thought of as subnormal is most inspiring. Many of his concepts accord well with the nurture group approach: the looking at the child's poor level of functioning in terms of their early experiences, the intervention at the developmental point that the child has reached, the idea that learning has to be 'mediated' by a close relationship with caring adults. 'For a child to learn, the teacher must interpose herself between the child and his surrounding world so that he can interpret it in a meaningful way' (Woolfson, 1993).

My view, delivered in the David Wills lecture in 1986, was that the success of this approach would have less to do with the 'instruments' themselves and more to do with the changed self-perceptions and motivation of pupils which resulted from the highly positive attitudes and focused expectations of their teachers, and from their offering new material which would have no associations of failure for the child. Blagg (1991) in his book, *Can We Teach Intelligence?*, is also of this opinion. He acknowledges that teachers and pupils involved in Instrumental Enrichment programmes become much more positive towards learning, in itself a considerable achievement, but he suggests that the skills gained on the special material do not of themselves generalize to other areas of learning such as literacy and numeracy.

Action in the classroom: 2. High/Scope

The second early intervention programme which has had central and local government support is High/Scope. This is one of the 'headstart' programmes which have had public funding in the USA to help pre-school children from deprived backgrounds to start formal education on a more equal footing with others. It was designed by a psychologist, Dr David Weikart, and a group of experienced teachers in Michigan, and was also heavily influenced by the work of Jean Piaget.

The project was monitored and evaluated over a period of 25 years (Berrueta-Clement *et al.*, 1984) and the important findings are that children going through the programme are likely to fare better than others from similar backgrounds in terms of employment, school attainments, further education, criminality, need for special education, and the incidence of teenage pregnancies. Thus the programme was seen to be effective in terms of cost to social agencies and in terms of human happiness.

The High/Scope pre-school programme was started in the UK in 1984 with the support of charities such as Barnardo's, some of whose staff had attended the pilot project, were favourably impressed, and reported changes in their colleagues' work with pre-school children, improvements in staff morale and positive comments from parents. The initial work was evaluated by a team of researchers led by Kathy Sylva (1986), and an Institute was established in 1990 which offers training courses to nursery and infant school teachers and to others who work with young children in social service, voluntary or private settings, and the use of the programme is spreading.[4]

There are striking similarities between the ideas behind High/Scope and the nurture group movement, even though they grew up in ignorance of each other's existence. To quote:

> In accepting the premise that children learn through the direct experiencing of objects, people and events, the adult's role in High/Scope is to provide an enabling environment which promotes active learning and which encourages children to think and talk about their actions. In a High/Scope environment the space is divided into well-defined areas containing materials that are logically organized and accessible so that children can work independently on activities they have planned themselves. The establishment and maintenance of a consistent daily routine enables children to develop awareness and control of their time as they begin to anticipate what will happen next. This control is necessary if children are to develop a sense of responsibility and to enjoy the opportunity to be independent. The daily routine includes a plan–do–review sequence in which the children are encouraged to make deliberate choices about their activities, to formulate and carry out their own plans and then to discuss the outcome with adults and peers. This 'review' aspect is a vital part of each session. (Sylva and Ilsley, 1992)

The emphasis on meeting the child at the stage he or she is at, the individual response to each child, the ordered way of working, the repetitions or rituals: these are all in common. The size of group is also comparable, with ten children to two adults being the desirable ratio. There can also be little doubt that children who get the positive, individual and structured approach of High/Scope are likely to benefit emotionally by the enhancement of their self-esteem. Equally, teachers or carers who have a clear plan of action for helping disadvantaged children, especially if they have support in reviewing progress, are likely to be of higher morale than teachers who are largely left to work on their own with children in difficulties. What is different in the explicit philosophy of the two movements is the nurture groups' emphasis on the child's total learning needs and the way in which these are closely linked to the child's early developmental experiences.

The High/Scope approach, and indeed the Instrumental Enrichment movement, at first took their theoretical position from the work of Piaget, a natural scientist by training, whose work started when he brought scientific techniques to the observation of the intellectual development of his own children. There is no evidence that he regarded emotional factors in children's development as being of importance, an attitude he held in common with most other theorists of intellectual development in his day. Piaget's work has had a great influence on teacher training over the past generation and hence on the way many teachers think about children's learning. His contribution can be briefly summarized by saying that he made people look at the way children's perceptions of the natural world and its rules differ from that of adults. This leads to the recognition that children learn better by doing, by experiencing for themselves, rather than simply by being instructed. (He was not, of course, alone in this insight; Froebel and Montessori, for example, also wrote extensively about the child's need to experience rather than simply to be told.)

It is probably true to say, however, that those of us who work with children at the extreme end of the continuum of emotional and behavioural difficulties do not find the Piagetian stages of development of great help in understanding the sources of a child's dysfunction. In fact, they can be seen as obscuring the importance of early emotional development in that they suggest that intellectual development is a natural process of maturation through different stages, like learning to walk. But it is a commonplace in work with many seriously disturbed children that their intellectual functioning is so severely affected by their early experiences that without expert help they do not go through normal stages of enquiry and interest in their surroundings; they do not achieve normal intellectual skills.

As well as differences in their underlying beliefs, there are also differences in the needs of the groups of children which High/Scope and nurture groups set out to meet. The first is designed as a boost to cognitive development, to help children who come from backgrounds which give them inadequate intellectual preparation for education. The second seeks to meet the needs of children who come to school having had such poor early developmental experiences that they have emotional or behavioural difficulties underlying their learning difficulties that are serious enough to make it impossible for them to stay in mainstream school.

There is nevertheless a great overlap between the thinking of the two groups and it is interesting that they are both becoming increasingly aware of the theories of the Russian psychologist, Vygotsky. Jaffey (1990), in her study of nurture groups in Enfield, discusses his theories on the connections between the development of language and of early relationships. 'Through speech children free themselves of many of the constraints of their environment. They prepare themselves for future activity; they plan, order and control their own behaviour as well as that of others.'

Sylva and Ilsley (1992), writing of the High/Scope approach to working with young children, state:

Vygotsky has written convincingly about the way adults move children on in their learning. Unlike Piaget who emphasized the learning that occurs when the lone child actively explores the physical environment, Vygotsky emphasised the learning which takes place when child and adult interact in a rich social and cultural context...The earliest and most important learning is assisted by a caring adult in an attitude of intimacy.

Feeling and thinking

Vygotsky died in 1934 so that his work has taken some time to reach the West. In his book, *Mind in Society* (1978), Vygotsky takes issue with Piaget for looking at the stages of intellectual development as though they proceed independently of the child's social, personal setting. It reads excitingly to those of us who have had to do the best we can to meet the pressing needs of children in difficulties from theoretical bases that have seemed inadequate when not actually wrong. It would be interesting to go on to speculate at length on the reasons for the relative scarcity of scientific and scholarly research on feelings, which few would deny are much more powerful in shaping the world than is rationality. Emotional phenomena, of course, are not easily measurable and so do not easily become the stuff of scientific endeavour. Perhaps psychology since it branched off from philosophy has been too concerned to establish itself as a scientific discipline by choosing problems that can be studied rigorously rather than the pressing questions that plague humanity.

Whatever the reasons, the recognition of the emotional aspects of teaching and learning have on the whole been remarkably neglected in the large body of educational research. Early emotional development has been largely seen as psychiatric territory, while educators have concentrated on intellectual development. This is a split reflected in the working practice of child guidance services a generation ago, where the educational psychologist looked at intellectual functioning and the psychiatrist looked at emotional states. Educational psychologists in the late 1950s were already beginning to challenge the narrowness of the idea of intellectual development proceeding more or less independently of the child's emotional circumstances, and the falseness of this position was certainly well recognized by the pioneers in special schools with 'maladjusted' children, as Bridgland (1971), for example, demonstrated in his account of the development of therapeutic education. But while 'the maladjusted' were thought of as a race apart, these insights were not on the whole generalized to the rest of the educational world.

Interest is now growing in the precise nature of the connection between emotional and intellectual development. At an applied level, work such as Greenhalgh's *Emotional Growth and Learning*, published in 1994, is beginning to focus attention on the underlying fears and feelings of children who need extra help with their emotional problems if they are to learn. At the level of scientific research, there is the journal *Cognition and Emotion*.[5] A special issue, 'Connections between emotion and understanding in development' (Dunn, 1995), focuses on areas that are highly relevant to understanding the educational development of all children, namely:

> the nature and developmental course of children's understanding of emotion; the development of children's understanding of mind; and the influence of a range of socialisation experiences...on children's social relationships and behaviour... Our data strongly suggests that a subjective experiential understanding of emotion precedes a subjective mentalistic understanding of cognitive states such as thoughts and beliefs. (p. 148)

> It is important to frame our developmental questions in terms of both cognitive and emotional considerations. (p. 200)

Or, as Dunn wrote earlier, 'the prevailing concentration on cognitive mechanisms as independent of emotional and motivational factors may not be providing the most useful framework for thinking about the development of social understanding' (Dunn, 1988). A theory of intellectual development that takes proper account of the centrality of feeling seems, therefore, well on its way. In the meantime, it is gratifying to record that after consultation with those of us who work with children with severe emotional and behavioural difficulties, there is explicit recognition in the documentation that accompanied the 1993 Education Act that 'the emotional development of children must continue to be a central concern for mainstream education' (para. 16).

A developmental view of children

It should be stressed that the first nurture groups were not set up to demonstrate a theoretical position. They were, as we have said, a response to increasing pressures on primary schools and they evolved as a joint project between a psychologist and teachers. Their great emphasis on the developmental foundations of learning derives primarily from the appalling case histories of so many of the children but is no doubt partly due to the fact that Marjorie Boxall worked in a multi-professional child guidance service. She had also trained as an educational psychologist in the multi-professional London Child Guidance Training Centre, where there was little emphasis on pedagogic skills and traditions, much more on psychiatric understanding of early family processes.

The work of John Bowlby on the nature of the early mother–child relationships was becoming widely known and influential. Beginning in 1944, with 'Forty-four juvenile thieves', his study of children who stole persistently, he focused attention on the early mother–child relationship and the processes by which children internalized feelings about themselves and attitudes towards others. His work was later challenged, partly because it was felt that he did not give sufficient weight to other influences in children's early development such as the support of the extended family, partly on the grounds that it was not sufficiently supported by experimental evidence. It is, of course, difficult to gather evidence rigorously about human development, the methods of natural science not being easily transferable to people; nor does the fact that something is unproven means that it is wrong, as some of his detractors claimed. What would by now be generally agreed was that he somewhat overstated the dangers of any separation of mother and child.

However, the central importance of the quality of early relationships, and their influence on the child's concepts of him or herself and others, remains. Rutter (1980), writing about the complexity of early development in *Maternal Deprivation Reassessed*, stated that recent years 'have seen the continuing accumulation of evidence showing the importance of deprivation and disadvantage as influences on children's psychological development. Bowlby's original arguments on that score have been amply confirmed.'

The change in ways of thinking about child development brought about by Bowlby and colleagues can hardly be over-stressed: the continuity of children's lives, the fact that what happens at one stage significantly influences the chance of success at the next; the idea that the child has a crucial point of view – all this was absent in earlier theories of childhood and in child-care practice. Anyone who doubts this should read *Empty Cradles* (Humphreys, 1994), a most moving account of the grief and emotional damage suffered by many children who were sent off, as young as four, to a new life in the Commonwealth. A philanthropic movement which was started in the 1870s to provide the Empire with children of British descent was still exporting children in public care as late as the 1960s to countries such as Canada, Australia and New Zealand.

The reasoning was that children from poverty-stricken homes in the UK would have a chance of a much better life in the more prosperous conditions abroad. It was not the practice to explain to the children what was happening, nor was it thought important to keep contact with parents or with siblings, so that many were sent without the knowledge of their families and lost all contact. It was not expected that they would be ill-treated, abused and exploited in their new homes, as some were. But even when this did not happen the effect of this breaking of the links with their homes and families, the lack of explanation of why their families had given them up, frequently had disastrous effects on their emotional development and ultimately their ability to manage their adult lives. It is unthinkable that children would be treated in this way now; and the shocked amazement which news of this work evoked demonstrates the shift in thinking.

Teachers' understanding

Marjorie Boxall found that teachers seized on the connection between their pupils' early family and social experiences and their current learning difficulties, readily accepted that effective intervention was possible, and with support were quickly able to redefine their task. Instead of seeing the child as failing and hence often feeling themselves to be failing, teachers quickly came to see that if the child could be taught at the level he or she had reached and offered the structures, the level of control, as well as warm emotional support appropriate to that stage, they moved on towards a better level of functioning, often quite rapidly. Once teachers gained confidence in the success of this approach they became involved and committed and their inventiveness flourished.

Concerns in 1996

Before ending, it should be noted that the experience of nurture groups and their effects on primary schools have relevance to two of society's current preoccupations: the continuing concern about educational attainments and about the social and moral development of children and young people. The government in 1996 is considering introducing national tests for five-year-olds and has published its expectations of what should have been achieved by the average child at the end of nursery school. As well as assessing children's knowledge of the world, their physical development and their creative development, the proposed assessment will look at the levels children should have reached in three other areas: language and literacy, mathematics and personal social development. To quote:

- Language and literacy; listen attentively and talk about experiences; use a growing vocabulary; make up stories and take part in role play; understand that words carry meaning and begin to associate sounds with syllables and letters; write their own name and recognize some familiar words.
- Mathematics; recognize and re-create patterns; use simple mathematical concepts and solve simple problems; recognize and use numbers to ten and be familiar with larger numbers; begin to show awareness of addition and subtraction and use the language involved.
- Personal and social development; be confident; show self-respect and be sensitive to others; establish relationships and work in a group or independently; dress and manage personal hygiene; learn to take turns and share; develop an understanding of right and wrong; experience cultural and religious events.[5]

Such assessments would identify children in need of extra help and it will be apparent by now that it is particularly in these areas of development that nurture group children lag behind, so clearly the principles on which nurture group work is founded are highly relevant.

Extra nursery school provision is often proposed as the solution to the problem of children coming into school at the age of five quite unready to benefit from formal education. There is no doubt that nursery education has by now overall proved its worth; the evidence for this is well summarized by Kathy Sylva (1994) in her authoritative report on nursery education:

The most rigorous studies show that high quality early education leads to lasting cognitive and social benefits in children which persist through adolescence and adulthood. The impact of early learning is found in all social groups but is strongest in children from disadvantaged back-grounds...(p. 94)

But Sylva also makes the point that national policy on nursery school provision,

falls short in a number of ways of providing an assurance of high quality – without which the benefits of pre-school education are seriously diminished. Moreover, many of those most in need, and most likely to benefit, miss out... The division of responsibility between the Health and Education Departments is a major difficulty – and so is the failure to grasp the principle on the integration of childcare and early learning. (p. 73)

This supports the conclusions of Eva Holmes' research, quoted in the first chapter, which showed that nursery education must be carefully focused, at the developmental stage of the child, if it is to help severely disadvantaged children to make real progress. Universally available nursery education based on the principles demonstrated to be effective by the work of the nurture groups would prevent much later failure, and is thus relevant to debates about academic and social and moral standards.

Commitment to school

If young children who cannot meet the demands of formal schooling are not given appropriate help quickly they fail to settle and to make reasonable academic progress. Much of the disaffection which occurs later doubtless has its roots in this early failure. A new study (Saunders, 1996; Bond and Saunders, 1999), based on the material collected by the National Child Development Study, shows that commitment to school is one of the important determinants of success in adult life. The data so far has demonstrated the influence of innate ability, educational privilege (i.e. private education) and parental social class on educational progress.

Analysing the information collected in 1991 on 17,000 33-year-olds – the children born in one week in March 1958 – Peter Saunders has found an interesting new correlation between success in adult working life and educational experience. Ability, as measured by tests at 11, continues to be the most important factor in their reaching professional, managerial and administrative occupations; it was five times more important than having had private education, and three times more important than parental class. But after ability the next most influential factor was shown to be commitment to school, as measured by school attendance rates, truancy rates, teacher assessments and motivation tests taken at the age of 16. Nobody reading the accounts of children in nurture groups can doubt that their commitment to school will increase significantly because of their experience of the groups. Saunders's study therefore further emphasizes the need for early intervention in a society that is concerned to make high-quality education accessible to all children.

Developing an understanding of right and wrong

One of the aims of the 1988 Education Act is to promote 'the spiritual (and) moral development of pupils at school and in society', a concern which properly continues to arouse great public debate. Whether young people today are morally better or worse than their predecessors is difficult to determine, nor is it a new question; nearly a thousand years ago Peter the Hermit is reputed to have said:

> The world is passing through troubled times. The young have no reverence for their parents: they are impatient of all restraint; they talk as if they alone know everything and what passes for wisdom with us is foolishness to them. (quoted in Rutter and Smith, 1995, p. 325)

But if it is difficult to measure changes in moral standards in the abstract, what can be shown is a considerable increase in behaviour which may be thought to reflect a decline. Rutter and Smith's wide-ranging survey of psychosocial disorders in young people between the ages of 12 and 26 shows that in the last 50 years there has been, across the whole of Western Europe, a marked rise in criminality, in depression and suicide, and in substance abuse, particularly among males. The causes for this are discussed and correlations shown: heavy unemployment among the young, relative poverty in an age of rising expectations, changes in family structures, earlier adolescence and prolonged dependence – all these may be relevant, but precise causal connections are difficult to establish.

What would be agreed by most people who work with the casualties in our society, with the addicts, the criminals, the seriously emotionally or behaviourally disturbed, is the frequency of unhappy, unsatisfactory childhoods, the lack of sustained and loving parental care. In their work they see people who have gone from failure to failure throughout their lives: the maldevelopment at one stage leading on to worse at the next. A report by Bob Johnson (1996), a psychiatrist who has worked in a prison unit for extremely violent men who have been convicted of offences such as rape and murder, describes graphically the immaturity that underlies their criminality. He describes the long and arduous process of social skills training by which men are given other ways of expressing themselves and are slowly convinced that there are better ways to manage their lives:

> I assisted in reducing violent assaults by 90 per cent... Something radical had changed, ... and the change was internal. These men had escaped from their childhood prisons... You have to believe that all violence comes from infantile 'logic' in adults who have never experienced friendly social exchange, and... don't believe it is possible. [He concludes] There is always a reason for human behaviour... underneath it all there is a logic, however twisted, infantile or irrational... the switch to turn the violence off is there, but it is often buried too deep to be readily accessible.

Little children are, by contrast, easy to reach and to influence. When they come into school they show clearly by their behaviour whether or not they have internalized a view of the world that is more than normally overwhelming, frightening or hostile; and whether or not they see themselves as adequate to meet the demands of school life, or feel threatened and under attack. It is relatively easy to help them while they are young but the longer the child continues with negative feelings and with the negative experiences these bring about, the greater the damage to his or her self-concept, the lower his or her self-respect and the greater the likelihood of later difficulties.

Nurture groups: their message

Nurture groups explicitly recognized that severely adverse early experiences affect every aspect of development and that they underlie much educational failure in mainstream schools. Such experiences leave social, emotional and intellectual deficits which nurture groups have demonstrated can be made good; that educational progress, in the widest sense, can be fostered. Teachers hearing about their work for the first time react with recognition and enthusiasm. Many, with or without their own experience as parents, already have all the insights needed to respond appropriately to children stuck at an earlier stage of development. All they need is a structure within which they can have the time to give each child the attention needed, and the confidence that comes from knowing that this approach has been proved to be effective.

Ordinary good teaching methods and class organization are easily adapted to the slower pace and individual needs of the nurture group children, as the work described in Enfield has demonstrated. The experience reported from the nurture groups which exist up and down the UK is that once teachers gain confidence they use themselves with increasing creativity and satisfaction. They are not asked to do more but to do what comes quite naturally to good teachers once they have been convinced of its importance, and once they are given the resources and the reassurance of official support.

Those of us who have followed the progress of nurture groups since their beginning and have introduced this way of thinking into work with teachers have no doubt of the power of their concepts. They have shown that early deprivation need not be compounded by educational failure; that many children showing signs of retarded development severe enough to warrant special placement can, with their help, remain in mainstream school. If all schools in areas of high social deprivation were run on the nurturing principles that come either from the presence of a nurture group, or from a close knowledge of their rationale and methods, the long-term benefit to children and to society would be immense.

NOTES
1. University of Bristol, Faculty of Education. 1972–87. Course tutor: Marion Bennathan.
2. The County of Avon Educational Psychology Service, for example, organized a public exhibition on the 1981 Act, with a handbook, which highlighted these issues and was the basis for many whole-school in-service days on educational success and failure.
3. Reported in the *Times Educational Supplement*, 18 August 1995.
4. High/Scope UK Institute, 190–2 Maple Road, London SE20 8HT.
5. Reported in *The Times*, p. 6, 10 January 1996.

Chapter 6

Nurture Groups in the New Century[1]

Marion Bennathan

This chapter will look at two aspects of what has been happening to nurture groups.

- First, there is the support for the concepts implicit in the work which has come from the growth in understanding of early childhood processes and their consequences for later development.
- Secondly, as is detailed in the Introduction, nurture groups have received wide support from the government and from many people concerned with education. The number of groups is growing rapidly which, while gratifying in that it demonstrates the power and attraction of the concept, brings some hazards as well as great opportunities. Work in progress and plans for future developments will be summarized.

Early Childhood

(a) Attachment processes

The centrality of attachment processes in human development has been increasingly accepted. In 1982, for example, the influential American Psychiatric Association (1982) in its *Diagnostic and Statistical Manual of Mental Disorders (DSM III)* listed *Reactive Attachment Disorder of Infancy* as a diagnostic category. At this point the criteria focused on babies in their first seven months who were showing 'a lack of developmentally appropriate signs of social responsivity', such symptoms as excessive sleep, poor muscle tone, failure to gain weight – also called 'failure to thrive'. The diagnosis was differentiated from other possible explanations such as mental retardation by the fact that 'the clinical picture is reversed shortly after institution of adequate caretaking'.

By 1994, the entry in the *Manual (DSM IV)* (American Psychiatric Association 1994) had greatly expanded. The condition was noted as starting before the age of five, its essential feature being 'markedly disturbed and developmentally inappropriate social relatedness' and its cause 'grossly pathological care'. It takes two forms, the first being the *Inhibited Type* in which the child 'persistently fails to initiate and to respond to most social interactions', and shows 'frozen watchfulness, resistance to comfort, or a mixture of approach and avoidance'. In the *Disinhibited Type* there is 'a pattern of diffuse attachments. The child exhibits indiscriminate sociability or a lack of selectivity in the choice of attachment figures.' The condition 'is associated with grossly pathological care that may take the form of persistent disregard of the child's basic emotional needs for comfort, stimulation or affection, persistent disregard of the child's basic physical needs; or repeated changes of primary caregiver that prevent formation of stable attachments.'

By now there is a considerable body of experimental work on attachment processes. The early research by Ainsworth has already been discussed. More recently there have been extensive studies of adults using the concept of attachment, described, for example, in *Attachment Theory: Social, Developmental, and Clinical Perspectives* (Goldberg *et al.*, 1995). One of the contributors, Mary Main, describes scales which have been developed which can reliably measure the 'internal working models of attachment' in adults and their effects on the capacity to make relationships. Importantly, included in this are parent–child relationships where damage can be shown to be trans-generational (Main in Goldberg *et al.*, 1995, pp. 407–74).

(b) Developments in neuropsychology

As well as being able to map out human development more accurately by attachment theory it is now becoming possible to find out by brain scans and by studying what is happening at cellular levels to have more precise information about activity in the human nervous system. This is not a topic which can be adequately discussed here but it needs to be highlighted because it has implications for education in general and for nurture groups in particular.

This was, for example, demonstrated at a conference in 1999 *Learning and the Brain*, in London at the Royal Institution. Chaired by its Director, Susan Greenfield, herself the author of *The Human Brain* (Greenfield 1997), the conference was addressed by eminent neuroscientists and educationists who considered what light cognitive psychologists and neuroscientists could throw on learning in the twenty-first century. Among the conclusions reported (Boxall *et al.*, 2000) were:

- self-esteem, confidence and motivation are strongly developed in babies;
- humans are intensely interactive;
- our genes do not impose a life sentence: the nature/nurture balance is towards nurture;
- the brain has considerable plasticity: neural connections are made after birth but prolonged stress can cause cell death and plasticity lessens with age;

- the relationship between early experience and later outcomes; if social competence has not been established by age six, children are at risk.

Robin Balbernie, reviewing developments in neuropsychology as a background to his study of infant mental health teams in the USA, writes:

> Trauma, chronically stressful or neglectful environments, will alter brain development so that the child becomes prone to emotional disturbance and less able to learn... It has been found that children... where the parent is emotionally unavailable, have a permanently higher level of [the hormone] cortisol, as do children who have been abused or those who have had depressed mothers in the first year of life... A response pattern that can be activated by fearful situations is the dissociative continuum. This is the freeze or surrender response, which is common in abused children, where signalling distress can lead to further threat. Such 'switching off' can be mislabelled as oppositional-defiant behaviour, so that more pressure is exerted, unaware that the child is feeling terrorised again, making it impossible for the child to produce the activity needed to comply with some demand. (Balbernie, 1999)

These findings have important implications for the management of children in difficulties in school. Translated into classroom terms, it means that some children cannot behave appropriately, cannot respond to management techniques that work with others. They need the opportunity to build up trusting relationships before they can begin to learn. Without that, the damage will continue and this will have consequences not only for their educational progress and that of others on whom their disturbance impinges, but also for their adult functioning. Given that opportunity, they can make the progress which will begin to reverse the damaging processes so far experienced.

This message of hope is reinforced by Ian Robertson, neuropsychologist. In his book *Mind Sculpture* he emphasizes the possibility of change for the better right through the human life span. On children's intellectual development, he has the following message for carers and teachers:

- talking to babies builds their intelligence;
- severe fear and stress can cause brain cells to shrink and even die;
- teaching children to read properly physically builds their brains;
- love grows the brain. (Robertson, 1999)

(c) Social policies, social attitudes

As has been noted earlier, the present UK government emphasizes the need for policies that prevent social exclusion. The policy paper *Social Inclusion: Pupil Support* (DfEE, 1999) puts the measures necessary to help pupils to progress in school 'in the context of wider action, nationally and locally, to prevent social exclusion – supporting local communities, encouraging employment and reducing crime'. That is to say, while education has a major role in providing the opportunities for good development, it can only do so with the co-operation of other agencies. If these are government funded, their support can be expected; current campaigns to reduce under-age pregnancies, to support families, to end child poverty, for example, are obviously helpful and relevant.

But government policies will not work if they do not command the support of the wider society, which is therefore essential if all children are to have the best chance of developing well. This means a widespread understanding of what enables children to grow up satisfactorily, of what lies behind the tragedies that occur in young lives. Explicit recognition is needed that young children are particularly vulnerable and can be damaged in ways that significantly affect their chances of a useful life; secondly it must equally be recognized that much early damage can be quite considerably reversed if the will is there.

Anyone who thinks that British society already has a high level of understanding of what causes children to go wrong should reflect on the recent public outcry about Mary Bell who at the age of ten strangled two little boys, aged three and four. Gita Sereny, an author with a record of important studies of children and others who commit serious crimes, recently published *Cries Unheard*, the sober and thoroughly researched story of Mary Bell's life (Sereny, 1999). Her aim, to discuss 'what is it, inside the human mind, the nerves, the heart, that first destroys or paralyses and then can recreate or reinstate morality and goodness', could hardly be more central to social concerns.

The book was written over several months, with long interviews which were tape-recorded and then painstakingly gone over again and again, so as to produce as accurate an account as possible. After the murder trial, Mary Bell was placed in Red Bank, a secure unit for delinquent adolescents. This did not offer psychotherapy and indeed the whole idea of helping children to come to terms with the events of their life was not in line with current thinking. Dr Dewi Jones, one of the support psychiatrists at the unit, told the author that before Mary arrived the staff were given a written directive on how to deal with her and were told that her background was unimportant for them to know about (since) a negative memory of the past...was best overcome by a positive approach to the present. 'This rejection of the significance of early childhood experience...was part of the established dogma...and deeply harmful to the care of troubled children.'

What Red Bank had, however, was a caring, intelligent director who, together with his devoted staff, treated Mary with kindness and respect. She herself thought that this was her salvation; what enabled her, after some years in a women's prison, to be released and to prove herself capable of leading a stable life, successfully mothering a daughter of her own.

Mary Bell herself did not seek publicity, indeed only agreed reluctantly to participate in the writing of the book because she had developed a relationship with the author over many years and because she was still concerned to make sense of her life. In particular she wanted to understand her tortured relationship with her mother, still asking herself, as do so many troubled children, 'What must I have done that she rejected me?'

The work was time-consuming, and stressful for both author and subject; painful for Mary Bell who still had great feelings of guilt about the boys she had killed and remorse for the sorrow she had brought to their families. Her early life was gone over in exhaustive detail. It was already known that her mother, unmarried and 17 at the time of her birth, had rejected her physically when she was placed, new-born, in her arms, that she had almost certainly made three attempts to kill her, that she had left her in the rather haphazard care of her extended family while she was away in another town working as a prostitute. It was only at the end of the many sessions that Mary could bring herself to reveal, in convincing detail, the full horror of her early life; that her mother had offered her to clients for oral sex, often forcing the reluctant child's head back very much in the way that Mary Bell later strangled the two small boys.

Sereny notes that after psychiatric examination before her trial she was labelled a psychopath. We must hope that with the greater understanding of child development in the last thirty years, such a diagnosis would no longer be applied. We must also hope that we have made progress in Sereny's second aim in writing the book, in looking 'very closely at the nature of communication we maintain with our children...crimes committed, not because of what they are, but because of what, unheard when early in their childhood they cried for help, they were made to be'.

Perhaps in professional circles we have achieved greater insight, and some better idea of how to intervene therapeutically. If so, we need to share this with the rest of society. The furore which followed the book's publication was not confined to the press, popular and otherwise, but went as far as discussion in parliament. It centred exclusively on Sereny's decision to give some of the profits from publication to Mary Bell, in recognition of her contribution to the writing of the book; on whether or not it was right for murderers to benefit from accounts of their crime. Of course there are serious issues about this but a society that is as knowledgeable about children as it ought to be would have had a different discussion: one which focused on the origins of criminality; on what society might have done better to protect children from such horrors.

(d) Reversing early damage

Nurture groups show that not all early damage to good development need be irreversible, a message that is being powerfully reinforced by a major study of Romanian children adopted by British families. This is the English and Romanian Adoptees (ERA) project at the London Institute of Psychiatry which is following the progress of children adopted from Romanian orphanages and hospitals whose plight came to worldwide attention as the Ceaucescu regime was brought to an end.

These children had spent their early months or years in extreme deprivation:

> the conditions in these institutions varied from poor to appalling. In most instances the children were mainly confined to cots; there were few, if any, toys or playthings; there was very little talk from caregivers; no personalized care-giving; feeding of gruel by bottles with large teats, often left propped up; and variable, but sometimes harsh, physical environments. Thus, washing often consisted of being hosed down with cold water. (Rutter *et al.*, 1998)

These circumstances resulted in children who, on entry to the UK, 'were severely developmentally impaired with about half below the third percentile on height, on weight and on head circumference, and on developmental quotient'. The hopeful finding is that those who were adopted before the age of six months had by the age of four years caught up with a comparable group of children adopted in the UK. The catch-up rate for children adopted after the age of six months was 'also impressive, but not complete'.

It is acknowledged that, perhaps because of the difficulties put in the way of people wishing to adopt children from Romania, the adopted parents were by and large a highly committed group, expecting difficulties and prepared to give devoted attention to their adopted children. 'Outcome in terms of catch-up in both physical development and cognitive functioning, was dramatic' (Groothues *et al.*, 1998).

That 'catch-up' occurred to a greater degree than expected is not to suggest that children can make full recoveries from extreme early conditions. A study was made (Rutter *et al.*, 1999) of the high incidence of 'quasi-autistic' patterns of development. Six per cent of the Romanian adoptees showed 'autistic-like patterns of behaviour', a further 6 per cent showed milder autistic features, which compares with the total absence of similar conditions in the group of British adoptees. The tentative conclusion was that the conditions noted 'seemed to be associated with a prolonged experience of perceptual and experiential privation, with a lack of opportunity to develop attachment relationships, and with cognitive impairment'. (It is interesting to note that, as recorded in Chapter 1, 'West Indian autism' was a psychiatric diagnosis applied to some of the traumatized children in Inner London in the 1960s and '70s.)

The ERA project seems likely also to enable 'attachment disorder' to be more precisely understood. O'Connor *et al.* (1999) reflect that 'despite the clear clinical and theoretical importance of attachment disorder, there are remarkably few systematic studies of attachment disorder behaviours or their etiology, course, and associated features'. Summarizing a long and careful discussion of the variability of symptoms, the authors write: 'Considered together, available findings on attachment disorder behaviours suggest that the critical causal factor may be the lack of a consistent and responsive caregiver (or small number of caregivers), or the opportunity of the child to form selective attachments.'

The ERA research may be expected to produce evidence that enhances our precise understanding of early childhood development. It will give emphasis to the importance of protecting children in the many social upheavals that take place all over the world. To come closer to home, it will be astonishing if it does not also support the general thesis of this book, which is that developmental damage to children in early childhood should be avoided as strenuously as possible and that when it is seen to have occurred, vigorous and skilled intervention should take place as quickly as possible.

Better than reversing early damage is preventing it from happening in the first place, and it may be hoped that current 'joined-up' multi-agency policies to ensure adequate support for children from birth onwards, will help to achieve this. What is needed is a wide recognition that good early experiences provide the foundations for later good development. As Marjorie Boxall wrote (Chapter 2)

> emotional, social and cognitive development in the earliest years is the product of adequate and attentive early nurturing care. It is a many-stranded, intermeshing, forward-moving, unitary learning process that centres on attachment and trust...It is the first stage of a developmental process through which the child builds up adequate concepts and skills, learns to interact and share with others and feel concern for them.

This, of course, is the starting point for nurture group work.

The success of nurture groups, and other initiatives which acknowledge the close connection of emotional and intellectual development, have a potential to contribute significantly to the overall good development of children in our society.

Nurture Groups: Work in Progress

A major development in promoting nurture groups has been the setting up of the University of Cambridge Nurture Group Project, as described in the Introduction. The Project Director, Paul Cooper, a much published writer on children with emotional and behavioural difficulties (e.g. Cooper, 1993; Cooper and McIntyre, 1996) and editor of the journal *Emotional and Behavioural Difficulties*, became interested in nurture groups after reviewing the first edition of this book. He wrote:

> the core message . . . is that schools will only achieve their most positive purposes for the children in their care when they inquire into and cater for the social, emotional and educational needs of all children. In order to do this they must listen to children and find ways of supporting them and nurturing them. Underpinning all of this is the value that is placed on children as individual human beings. Without this sense of value all of the strategies in the world are worthless. This book is . . . a palpable demonstration of what it means to value children in this way. (Cooper, 1997)

The Nurture Group Consortium had already been set up to enhance the promotion of the groups and was delighted to have the support of the Project which began work in September 1998. The Project has a major research function to which Consortium members contribute some consultation. Its staff take responsibility for the organization of the Certificate Course, members of the Consortium contributing to the teaching. Other training, such as day events, lectures and workshops, are organized by the Consortium which also takes responsibility for publicity and for publications. The two groups keep in close and regular contact and share information about developments so that it seems more sensible to organize this section mainly under topics rather than attribution.

First, however, a summary of the research carried out so far and published in October 1999 in the Research Project Report *The Nature and Distribution of Nurture Groups in England and Wales* (Cooper, Arnold and Boyd, 1999) is appropriate. Further material from the Report will be quoted under topic headings.

The Research Project Report

The findings on which the Report is based come from a survey by questionnaire sent to all LEAs in England and Wales, to which 63 responded, and also from information collected by the research team in the course of training and consultative activities. The aims of the research, in this its first stage, were:

(a) To generate detailed knowledge of the distribution of nurture groups in England and Wales.

(b) To define the nature of nurture groups in terms of practical and organizational arrangements.

(c) To generate and pilot evaluation techniques that will assess the effectiveness of nurture groups.

(d) To contribute to the development of nurture groups through the dissemination of information, consultancy and advice that will be of value to persons seeking to set up nurture groups. (Project Report, p. 8)

In brief, the replies gave information that pointed the way to further action:

(a) More nurture groups existed than had been known about; 16 of the 63 responding LEAs indicated that they already had nurture groups, some 11 more that they were proposing to set them up and all but one expressed interest in being kept informed of the development of groups; many wanted more information about nurture groups and over half the respondents asked for further information about training. There was widespread awareness of the need for early intervention and inclusion with many LEAs reporting projects to achieve this, few of which had been set up within an evaluative framework.

(b) What was meant by 'a nurture group' was seen to be by no means clear and will be discussed in the next section.

(c) Evaluation techniques are taught as part of the Certificate Course; valuable information is accruing, some of which will be discussed under 'The use of the Boxall Profile'.

(d) The dissemination of information is an ongoing and expanding process which will be discussed later.

What is a 'nurture group'?

Since the survey in late 1998 and indeed since the Report was published in October 1999, many more LEAs in England and Wales have asked for information and consultation and are in process of setting up groups, and there is active interest from Scotland, Ireland, Canada, New Zealand, the USA and the Netherlands.

Keeping count of new nurture groups is something still to be tackled effectively. One of the difficulties in doing so is that not all groups are set up with the knowledge of the Consortium, nor if known would they be accepted as genuine 'nurture groups'. There are important questions of definition and linked to that questions of quality assurance. A large fund of experience has been built up in the ILEA and in Enfield. This is expanding rapidly as it is shared with the students on the Cambridge Certificate Course who then put their new skills into practice and contribute valuable feedback to the Project. It is a concern that groups are being set up with no reference to this expertise, which includes knowledge of possible pitfalls. The Consortium is addressing the problem in various ways. It is, for example, seeking to get a clear acceptance of what is and what is not a 'nurture group' both by acquiring some legal control over the use of the word and by defining criteria more precisely.

This is not to suggest that the successful ways of working developed in Inner London and in Enfield are inflexible and unchangeable. There was already variation in ILEA, some groups, for example, meeting not for the major part of the day but only for morning sessions. Groups in Newcastle, as described earlier, were set up not as an integral part of a school but as an area resource. Schools change, local needs vary and, in the words of the Report, 'it will be an important part of the further research to evaluate the relative effectiveness of different nurture group models, as well as comparing the effectiveness of these models with alternative forms of provision'. The Project Report offered four descriptions:

(a) classic 'Boxall' nurture groups, which accord in all respects with the model established by Marjorie Boxall (see Bennathan and Boxall, 1996);

(b) variants which differ in structural and/or organizational features from the Boxall model, but clearly adhere to the core principles which underpin the Boxall nurture groups in terms of a commitment to the provision of early learning experiences through a nurturing approach which can be elucidated in terms of Bowlby's attachment theory;

(c) groups which bear the name 'nurture group', or are claimed to be variants of the nurture group concept, but which do not conform to either the Boxall model or Boxall principles;

(d) groups which bear the name 'nurture group', or are claimed to be variants of the nurture group concept, but which are presented in terms which contravene, undermine and/or distort the defining principles of the original nurture groups. (Project Report, p. 8)

To give three examples of groups which are not acceptable as nurture groups, in recent months the Consortium has come across groups at secondary level which function on an ad hoc basis, pupils who are having difficulty managing in class being sent to them for time out without much assessment of need or agreed procedures of entry and return. One such group had a banner stretched across its room on which was written 'Welcome To Our Nurture Group' which seemed unlikely to enhance adolescent self-esteem. The well-intentioned staff working there felt that they were making little progress; they had no precisely defined aims or rationale; they did not know where the nurture group concept originated.

Another group which claims the name is run by an independent therapist and a school nurse, meets in school for play therapy during the lunch hour on three days a week. It believes in the use of 'regression therapy', and puts great faith in Piaget's developmental principles, neither of which are used in nurture group work. A third group is for pre-school children, a health-service facility for children proving very difficult to manage at home. The children attend for one day a week and the programmes are based on behaviour modification principles, i.e. the child is repeatedly shown the behaviour expected with rewards for conforming and 'extinction' of the bad behaviour by, where possible, ignoring. The parents observe and follow the advice of the staff.

This group reportedly achieves success. It is not, however, based on nurture group principles. This is not to say that behaviourist approaches – ignoring the bad behaviour, rewarding the good – are banned in nurture groups. They can be useful but they have to be used in the context of an empathetic relationship: understanding the child's perceptions, building up trust, conveying to the child that she or he is valued and moving on as the child is ready. Jackson's account of Jim, aged three, will illustrate the important difference in the two approaches:

> On some days Jim comes into the nursery class already anxious and unsettled. He pushes and hits other children, moves from one activity to another without settling, often interrupting or spoiling the activities of others. The school has an excellent behaviour policy... [but] with a small number of children behaviourist strategies are not enough. Nurture techniques are often very different from behaviourist approaches, sometimes apparently contradictory; for example, comforting a child who is unsettled might be seen as reinforcing the undesirable behaviour. Nurture approaches are about responding to a child at the level of relationships and emotions. (Jackson, 1999)

As well as failing to follow nurture group concepts, the three groups described are not primarily concerned with 'accessing the curriculum' or, as we might say, helping children to learn. So they do not conform to either variant (a) or (b) above. Without more evidence it is not possible to say whether they merit a (c) or a (d).

Criteria

Clearly, if groups are not properly set up and fail, first, there is a waste of resources, secondly, the whole concept may be brought into disrepute. To help to a better understanding of what is involved in running a nurture group, the Project Report offered an extensive list of criteria, namely, that nurture groups should:

(a) be located clearly within the policies and structures of an LEA/school continuum of special educational needs provision, either as an integral part of an individual school or as a resource for a cluster of schools;

(b) ensure that children attending the nurture group remain members of a mainstream class where they register daily and attend selected activities;

(c) have a pattern of attendance whereby children spend a large part of each day in the nurture group or attend for substantial regular sessions;

(d) ensure that the National Curriculum is taught;

(e) be taken full account of in school policies, participate fully, and be fully considered in the development and review of policies;

(f) offer short or medium term placements, usually for between two and four terms, depending on the child's specific needs, which have been determined on the basis of systematic assessment in which appropriate diagnostic and evaluative instruments have been used, with the aim always being to return the child to full-time mainstream provision;

(g) supply a setting and relationships for children in which missing or insufficiently internalised essential early learning experiences are provided;

(h) be staffed by two adults working together modelling good adult relationships in a structured and predictable environment, where children can begin to trust adults and to learn;

(i) offer support for children's positive emotional and social growth and cognitive development at whatever level of need the children show by responding to them in a developmentally appropriate way;

(j) place an emphasis on language development through intensive interaction with an adult and with other children;

(k) provide opportunities for social learning through cooperation and play with others in a group with an appropriate mix of children;

(l) using appropriate diagnostic and assessment instruments, monitor and evaluate the effectiveness of the nurture group provision in promoting the positive social, emotional and educational development of each child;

(m) promote the active involvement of mainstream staff in the life of the nurture group;

(n) be staffed by adults who have and promote a positive attitude towards parents/carers of all children and encourage their involvement in activities supportive of the nurture group programme. (Project Report, p. 6)

Nurture groups at secondary level?

Nurture groups have, for the most part been set up at infant school level (ages 4+ to 7), although one of the first nurture groups set up in London in 1970 was in a junior school (ages 7 to 11) and was regarded by the staff as highly successful. Logically, however, it makes sense for the groups to be established so that they protect children as early in their school careers as possible from the experience of failure. As the groups spread in ILEA the majority were at infant level, which is also the case in Enfield. In some LEAs, as the success of their recently established groups becomes apparent, the question is arising as to whether they would work at secondary level.

At first sight, this seems unlikely; the replicating of early mother–child relationships central to nurture group thinking does not easily translate to adolescence. Yet the nurture group coordinator of a group of schools in a deprived area of Staffordshire, having seen the rapid improvement in children attending the primary age groups, has set up a group of 12 to 13-year-old pupils, all at serious risk of exclusion, which meets for one morning a week. Difficulties experienced during the previous week are discussed; the two staff and, with encouragement, the other pupils listen acceptingly and suggest different approaches. Then there is the traditional nurture group 'breakfast'. At first, this was a hot drink and biscuits. On reflection, the staff changed to having toast; they thought that the bother of having to prepare it, and passing round the butter and jam, gave group members more opportunity for helping each other and being thanked, a new experience for many of them. After breakfast, there is some creative work, such as drama or painting. It is not claimed that this is a nurture group, but as one of the staff said, 'We have a nurture group in our heads, and that supplies the inspiration.' After less than a term, colleagues in the school are beginning to notice significant improvement in the pupils' response in the normal classes.

Some secondary school staff wished to enrol on the Cambridge Course and, with due warning about its early years bias, were accepted and have been pleased with the development of their understanding and skills with their pupils with EBD. This was noted in the Project Report:

> we are reassured and impressed by the sensitivity and thoughtfulness of the staff who are embarking on this pioneering development. The central challenge facing these individuals is the need to discover age appropriate strategies for delivering the nurture group approach to these older children. Clearly, the activities and forms of interaction that are appropriate in the reception or Year 1 classroom are not appropriate for children of secondary age, even if their underlying needs are the same.

The use of the Boxall Profile

What staff at all stages are increasingly discovering is the usefulness of the Boxall Profile, whose development in ILEA is described in Chapter 2. The new *Handbook* (Bennathan and Boxall, 1998) contains the Profile itself, with permission to copy it, instructions for its use and discussion of the significance of its findings. There are also examples of its use over time with four nurture group pupils which show how it helps staff to identify areas of difficulty more exactly and to prepare focused individual education plans.

The Profile was designed and standardized for use with children aged 3–8 but, the scoring being based on the teacher's knowledge of what is appropriate to each age group, it has been found to be successful in use at any age. What teachers find it does is to help them to look at their pupils with more insight. As the head of secondary education in a residential special school wrote: 'It is only too easy for teachers to start labelling children as aggressive or psychopathic. The Profile makes everybody think about what lies behind the behaviour and it stimulates discussion about what we might do next with a child in serious difficulties.' After a training session at a secure unit for adolescents, the staff were unanimous in finding it helpful. One commented: 'The Profile gives us a structure to look at young people's behaviour, to discuss it constructively and to plan together what we can do about it. We have not discussed our pupils as positively as this before.'

The Special Educational Needs Coordinator (SENCO) in a large secondary school wrote of it (Panter 1999):

> The Boxall Profile is a very useful tool to identify those pupils who need intervention that does not just deal with their behaviour; who will not respond unless their underlying emotional needs are recognized and acknowledged. As such it helps the Learning Support Department to plan the intervention most likely to succeed. We also find it a useful tool to demonstrate to other staff what a pupil will or will not respond to; whether behaviour management strategies, such as assertive discipline or other in-class strategies, will work or whether some withdrawal from the class and support to re-enter it is necessary.
>
> This work is in its infancy but it is already confirming our belief that it is a useful tool which prevents 'papering over the cracks' of a real emotional need only to find that this erupts later *with a vengeance.*

The Profile is demonstrated at every training event as well as used on the Certificate Course so that it has by now been discussed with several hundred people, on whose response it will be useful to report briefly. As is described in Chapter 2, the Profile is an integral part of the development of nurture group work. It grew out of the needs expressed by ILEA teachers to have a more systematic way of describing and monitoring children in nurture groups; its checklist items were based on their observations of children.

It has two sections. The first, 'Developmental Strands', consists of 34 items which describe different aspects of the early developmental processes and show how the pupil has come through these. The second, the Diagnostic Profile, also based on 34 items, sorts out the responses into three clusters: *self-limiting features*, e.g. 'avoids, rejects or becomes upset when faced with a new and unfamiliar task, or a difficult or competitive situation'; *undeveloped behaviour*, e.g. 'restless or erratic; behaviour is without purposeful sequence, continuity or direction'; *unsupported development*, e.g. 'lacks trust in the adults' intentions and is wary of what they might do; avoids contact or readily shows fear'.

Groups new to the Profile have no difficulty in relating its explanations to children they have worked with; it clearly gives them an immediately accessible entry to understanding what lies behind the child's behaviour. The value of this is inestimable. The apparently senseless behaviour of pupils with EBD can be threatening to the most competent of teachers. If the adult then responds with anger, with confusion, even with fear, pupils may either become ever more anxious as their capacity to evoke negative responses, their 'badness', is once again recognized, or they may be reinforced in believing that the defensive/hostile responses they have developed are effective protection. In neither case will the child's maladaptive response be changed, indeed it is likely to be confirmed.

With the insights that come from using the Profile, teachers develop greater confidence. As one experienced nurture group teacher said: 'Confronted with a child whose anxiety-provoking behaviour seems to make no sense, the Profile is where you start. It gives you insights and suggests points of entry into the child's world.' Staff begin to learn the art of accepting the child while rejecting the behaviour, which is the essence of successful work with emotionally damaged children. With greater understanding they learn not to feel threatened by unresponsive pupils; they learn that an aggressive façade often conceals a great deal of insecurity and fear. This growth of confidence releases energy and creativity in staff, allowing them to use themselves better and with much greater satisfaction. This may be the single most powerful feature in the success of nurture group work and it is relevant at all stages of education.

The Profile's relevance to social policy

In one LEA where nurture groups are well established, staff are becoming aware of what they think is a preponderance, possibly an increase, of children scoring heavily on the third cluster of Section II of the Profile, that named 'unsupported development' whose component parts are sub-clusters V to Z:

V. avoids/rejects attachment;
W. has undeveloped/insecure sense of self;
X. shows negativism towards self;
Y. shows negativism towards others;
Z. wants, grabs, disregarding others.

Such tendencies if they persist are clearly likely to lead to long-term antisocial attitudes, so that the effective early intervention that nurture groups bring about is highly relevant to policies for treating delinquents. Mitchell Yell, working in the USA on violence in schools (Yell *et al.*, 1999), discusses the outcomes of different treatment approaches. His view is that 'behaviour reduction' (i.e. punishment) approaches show very little evidence of success.

> Such interventions may be effective in momentarily controlling problem behaviour but the behaviour reappears when the student moves from his or her protected setting into the general education or community setting ...Punishment orientated approaches involve very little learning... punishment and control have been abysmally unsuccessful in preparing students with EBD to function successfully in society.

It is already the experience of nurture group staff that children who score heavily on the 'unsupported development' cluster of the Profile are more difficult to help than those scoring heavily on the 'undeveloped behaviour' cluster. It is likely that the latter are children 'who have had too little help to provide them with the inner resources to relate to others and engage at an age-appropriate level. ...they have a readily available potential for attachment and are likely to respond well to an early level relationship and appropriate experiences'.

For the former 'the suggestion is that the child has suffered a profound lack of early nurturing care, probably associated with intrusively negative experiences'. From V through to Y

> insecurity and fear give way to a thrust for survival. As a protection against hurt and to maintain self-regard, increasingly alienated and negative behaviour appears. Children showing marked features of negativism towards others, as in Y, are motivated by anger, sometimes by rage, as they make their own way; their anti-social behaviour may become an increasingly well-organized, internalised pattern that brings them power and satisfaction and is thus self-perpetuating and motivating.

The implications of this for social inclusion policies are considerable and merit systematic research. If the Profile is used to identify children whose failure to progress in school has its origins in this pattern of maldevelopment, it could be the spur to much more focused intervention out of school than already exists. It could also support the position of almost everybody who works with children with EBD that punishment has no useful place in their management. We would include in punitive practices the exclusion of pupils from school which still plays a central role in government policy and which ought to be replaced, when it is really necessary, by the much less damaging planned transfer to appropriate provision. Clearly, making inclusion work for the good of the child deserves all the help it can get.

The inclusion/exclusion debate

The real appeal of nurture groups for those of us who work with vulnerable children is that, as well as helping them to prosper in mainstream, they demonstrably benefit the children they serve, which ought, of course, to be the first aim of all provision. But it must be admitted that a large part of their appeal to fundholders and to administrators is that they support the policy of inclusion. Yet even nurture groups are opposed by senior management in some LEAs on the grounds that anything which 'segregates', i.e. removes a child from the classroom, is wrong in itself, whatever help is thereby given to the child. This smacks to some of us of dogma, of looking at the belief rather than at the child. A special needs adviser in an inner city LEA, defeated in her attempts to introduce nurture groups, said her senior officer, 'He thinks it's all right for the child to spend the day in disgrace in the head teacher's room, but a nurture group would be harmful.'

As the Project Report says,

> the physical inclusion of a particular pupil in a mainstream classroom is not necessarily synonymous with the active engagement of that pupil in the social and educational life of the classroom. Some children manage to pass through school 'shrouded in a cloak of invisibility' (Pye, 1988). Other, often more disruptive, pupils may be marginalised as a result of peer rejection and the implementation of interventions designed to control their scope for disruption. (Project Report, pp. 5–6)

Clearly, as inclusion pressure groups claim, 'segregation' can work against the child's best interests. Removal from the mainstream class can be done with hostility, can stigmatize, so that the pupils in the special provision and sometimes their teachers are marginalized and outside the life of the school. If nurture groups are to contribute to the sort of inclusion that benefits the child, it is important, as has been frequently said, that the group is a highly regarded, well-understood, integral part of the school. As an ILEA head teacher, quoted in Chapter 3, said, 'The best way to set up a "sin-bin" is to set up a nurture group without the support of the whole school staff.'

If nurture groups are set up in the ways recommended, they are not only 'inclusive' in the best meaning of the term, they also contribute to the inclusive ethos of the whole school. This was noted as long ago as 1984 in the evidence of ILEA head teachers to the Fish Committee, quoted earlier. Also, it is frequently reported that the groups are so well accepted in their schools that other pupils ask to be admitted, to which many schools respond by allowing the group children to invite a special friend in, or by inviting children from the mainstream classes in for tea or for a birthday party.

An interesting reaction was reported recently from an OFSTED inspector, who rather upended the inclusive lobby's claim that all 'segregation' is bad by asking, under the heading of equal opportunities, if it were fair to the rest of the pupils for the nurture group children to have such a privileged life. The answer given was that the group was 'the warm heart of the school', that all the pupils benefit from its existence and that all of them are invited to visit it, however briefly.

Where next?

The Nurture Group Consortium and the Project are moving fast to keep up with the exciting speed of development.

Training opportunities

These are being expanded. The Cambridge Certificate Course has been consistently fully subscribed since it started and other modes of in-depth training are being considered. In-service day courses, lectures and workshops have taken place in all parts of the UK, from the Isle of Wight to Scotland, from Northern Ireland to East Anglia. All events are evaluated and all evaluations have been extremely positive.

Building up a network

Building a network of communication for people interested in nurture groups is starting. The twice yearly Newsletter of the AWCEBD has since 1997 had a section on nurture groups. A questionnaire has just been circulated to all known nurture groups to establish what is now wanted; possibly a separate news-sheet will emerge. A website (www.educ.cam.uk/nurture) has also been set up.

Information

Information is vital as is the sharing of experience. The AWCEBD Newsletter publishes articles from people in nurture group work, one in the Winter 1999 issue by a learning support assistant, whose role is vital to the good running of the group. Most movingly, a mother allowed us to publish (Summer 2000 issue) a detailed account of the transformation of her son at home and at school after his year in a nurture group. This was written to her LEA when she heard that continued funding was not certain. Although her son was ready to move on she wanted to make sure that the group continued for other children in need.

Lucas (1999) wrote on the effects on her headship of a school in a privileged area that came from running a nurture group in an area of severe deprivation; of the insights gained which enabled her to create what was recognized as a 'nurturing school'. Information on the practicalities of running nurture groups, pamphlets, handbooks, are needed and are in preparation.

Funding

Funding for nurture groups is seen by many LEAs as a stumbling block to the setting up of groups. What is in danger of happening at present is that special funding is provided for a limited period, sometimes one or two years. Then just as the group staff have built up their expertise and the host school is beginning to reap the benefit, threats to funding arise. Whether more central funding is necessary or whether LEAs and schools could achieve more by reorganizing their budgets needs to be discussed.

'Accessing the curriculum'

This continues to be a concern for those considering setting up nurture groups. The answer is surely that for some children the curriculum will never be accessed unless the child gets help to put in the missing stages in learning. Teachers know this; perhaps their main need is to be helped to justify what they do as they prepare for inspection. Experience is that the once the children settle down and attach themselves to the staff the necessary foundations for learning are put in and learning takes place. *The Nurture Group Curriculum* (Enfield, 2000) is helpful on this.

Working with parents

In looking at the origins of children's difficulties, there has been an emphasis on what has gone wrong in the early attachment processes. It must be reiterated that the stated ethos of nurture groups is not to be judgemental about parents. Child-rearing is full of hazards: social circumstances such as housing and employment levels can support or sabotage. Some children are from birth more difficult to rear than others. The consistent finding is that parents welcome their child's placement in a nurture group when they would for the most part resist the suggestion of special school. The group also protects them from the painful experience of their child being excluded from school. This not only causes great practical problems for families who are usually already over-burdened but is extremely damaging to parental self-esteem; perhaps a final proof of failure and worthlessness.

The name 'nurture group' is thought by some to be patronizing to parents and schools have traditionally made vigorous efforts to have the class known by some other name such as 'Rainbow Class'. In fact, experience is beginning to suggest that parents who know the class as the nurture group do not find this offensive. They know their child needs help: they welcome the support they and their child are offered. One of the research interests of the Cambridge Project is currently to consult parents on their feelings about nurture groups, so more will be known about this before long.

It is worth noting that when nurture groups first started in Inner London, some of them tried to work extensively with parents as well as with the children. This was found to need more staff resources than were available. There are also complex issues in some very troubled families about children having the right to some area of their lives where they can develop in peace. It may be that a better way to achieve 'joined-up' support for children is for there to be more explicit working links with other agencies.

Multi-agency work

There is repeated emphasis in all pronouncements on social policy for official agencies to work together for the good of children. Schools are certainly well aware that they need help in managing children with EBD. As the Project Report says of LEA responses to the questionnaire:

A particularly striking aspect... is the shared recognition that effective responses to the problem of EBD in schools have to go *beyond* schools in terms of involving professionals and organizations outside the education field. They also have to involve parents and in some cases focus on pre-school and out of school settings. These perceptions suggest that many LEAs are engaging with the complexities of EBD as a multi-faceted phenomenon which is only partly a school based educational problem. The prominence of multi-disciplinary and family based work suggests a continuity with important aspects of the nurture group approach.

Many schools already have built up close working relationships with social workers where the child is 'at risk' in the family or is already in public care. There is scope for this to be developed and it is one of the aims for work in the future.

Research

Research is ongoing. Several students who have completed the Cambridge Course are going on to doctoral dissertations on aspects of their work with nurture groups. Cooper and Lovey (1999) carried out a survey of the views of staff with experience of nurture groups. There were four questions, given below, (Q). Space does not allow more than brief excerpts from the replies, (R), below, but these will give the flavour of a highly favourable response.

> Q1. *How do NGs differ from other support for children with special educational needs?*
>
> Ri. The support is immediate, educationally focused, accessible when needed and flexible.
>
> Rii. NGs start from the true recognition of where the child is at – and valued as such; and enable children to reach where they should be.
>
> Q2. *How would you describe the child who would benefit from time in a NG?*
>
> Ri. One with emotional/cognitive delay due to confused environment/ attachment experience.
>
> Rii. Any child who is failing to thrive in the educational climate provided by the school.
>
> Q3. *What would you expect this child to gain from the group?*
>
> Ri. Marked increase in general competence and autonomous functioning, improved social relationships, concern for others, greater self-awareness and self-esteem, emergence of reflective behaviour and self-regulation.
>
> Rii. Successful experiences at any level; good self-image; an ability to make and sustain peer/adult relationships.
>
> Q4. *How do you think the school is affected by having a NG?*
>
> Ri. In the school as a whole, optimism and constructive attitudes replace negativism and rejection of the children.
>
> Rii. Parents feel they have been given support and full recognition of the child's needs without exclusion from mainstream.

The authors conclude 'there was confidence that it was possible for the NGs to make a major difference to schools that were, at the same time, committed to all the policy developments and "innovations" that have assailed schools in England and Wales over the last year and a half'.

The Cambridge Nurture Group Project

The Project is well into the second phase of its research, and as we go to press there is an announcement of substantial funding from the Nuffield Foundation, a twofold benefit in that it recognizes the importance of the work, and enables it to continue. As to future aims and plans, let the Project Report speak for itself:

> The fact that there is enthusiasm among educators to extend the nurture group approach . . . is an indication of the power of the approach to strike chords with teachers from all phases. What is also clear, however, is that the attraction of nurture groups can at present (in common with much provision for children with emotional and behavioural difficulties) owe little to knowledge of quantifiable evidence of their efficacy. Our study reveals only limited evidence of evaluation, either existing or planned. The lack of evaluation evidence might be seen to support the idea that nurture groups appeal to intuition and common sense. Experienced and informed practitioners can see both the need for and the logic of the nurture group approach. On the other hand, intuition and common sense alone are an unreliable basis for educational policy and practice. For this reason it is essential that the future development of nurture group provision be informed by systematic evidence of the effectiveness of the approach. Without such evaluation data it is hard to see how the continued use of any form of provision can be justified in preference to another in a climate of competing priorities and financial constraint.
>
> To this end the project team has identified a range of evaluation instruments and a strategy for applying them to nurture group provision. The instruments were trialled in the Summer term (1999) and it is intended to begin a national evaluation programme in the Autumn of 1999. Funding has already been secured from the DfEE and the Calouste Gulbenkian Foundation to support this initiative. There has already been considerable interest expressed by a number of LEAs in working with the team on this evaluation project. Also, the nurture group training places a strong emphasis on the need for nurture groups to be self-evaluating, and provides guidance on this. Key questions to be addressed in the proposed two-year extension to the current project are:
>
> (a) What is the relative effectiveness of different models of nurture groups for the social, emotional and educational development of children who attend them?
> (b) What is the impact of nurture groups on host schools in terms of mainstream teachers' perceptions and practice?
> (c) What are children's perceptions of and attitudes towards nurture groups?

(d) What are parental perceptions of and attitudes towards nurture groups?
(e) What are the effects of nurture groups on parents' approaches to child rearing?

An additional concern of this study will be to explore the nature and value of nurture group approaches when applied to students of secondary school age.

Such a project will have the benefit of supplying invaluable data to LEAs currently employing nurture groups, LEAs setting up nurture groups and LEAs contemplating the development of their EBD provision. The present situation, in which many LEAs are developing nurture groups from scratch, is also advantageous in that it provides us with the opportunity to track the development of these nurture groups from their inception.

And finally...

Those of us who have worked to promote nurture groups over the past several years welcome the careful research that is now being undertaken. We have no doubt that it will confirm what we have seen in the responses of the many teachers and others concerned to do their best for vulnerable children to the value of the nurture group approach.

The first edition of this book ended with the bold assertion that 'if all schools in areas of high social deprivation were run on the nurturing principles that come either from the presence of a nurture group, or from a close knowledge of their rationale and methods, the long-term benefit to children and to society would be immense'. In the four years since that appeared significant progress has been made.

NOTES
1. My thanks are due to Marjorie Boxall and Mel Sabshin for reading and constructively commenting on this chapter.

References

Ainsworth, M.D. *et al.* (1978) *Patterns of Attachment.* New Jersey: Erlbaum.

American Psychiatric Association (1982) *Diagnostic and Statistical Manual of Mental Disorders (DSM-III).* APA, Washington DC.

American Psychiatric Association (1994) *DSM- IV.* APA, Washington DC.

Association of Metropolitan Authorities (1995) *Reviewing Special Educational Needs.* London: AMA, p. 25.

Balbernie, R. (1999) 'Infant mental health', *Young Minds Magazine* **39**, Mar/Apr.

Bennathan, M. (1992) 'The care and education of troubled children', *Therapeutic Care and Education* **1**(1): 37–49.

Bennathan, M. (1995) 'Listening to children in school'. In Davie, R. and Galloway, D. (eds), *Listening to Children in Education.* London: David Fulton Publishers.

Bennathan, M. and Boxall, M. (1996) *Effective Intervention in Primary Schools: Nurture Groups,* 1st edn. London: David Fulton Publishers.

Bennathan, M. and Boxall, M. (1998) *The Boxall Profile: Handbook for Teachers.* Maidstone: AWCEBD.

Bernstein, B. (1970) 'Social class, language and socialisation', unpublished paper quoted in Bruner, J. (1974) *The Relevance of Education,* p. 165. London: Penguin.

Berrueta-Clement, J.R. *et al.* (1984) *Changed Lives: The Effects of the Perry Pre-school Program on Youths through Age 19.* Monographs of the High/Scope Press, Ypsilanti, Michigan, No. 8.

Blagg, N. (1991) *Can We Teach Intelligence? A Comprehensive Evaluation of Feuerstein's Instrumental Enrichment Program.* Brighton: Lawrence Erlbaum Associates.

Blank, M. and Solomon, F. (1969) 'How shall the disadvantaged child be taught?', *Child Development* **40**: 47–61.

Bond, R. and Saunders, P. (1999) 'Routes of success: influences on the occupational attainment of young British males', *British Journal of Sociology* **50**(2): 217–49.

Bowlby, J. (1944) 'Forty-four juvenile thieves: their characters and home life', *International Journal of Psycho-Analysis.*

Bowlby, J. (1951) *Maternal Care and Mental Health.* World Health Organization, London: HMSO.

Boxall, M. (1976) *The Nurture Group in the Primary School.* ILEA (Chapter 2 of the present volume).

Boxall, M., Holmes, E. and Lucas, S. (2000) 'Learning and the brain', *AWCEBD Newsletter,* Summer.

Bridgland, M. (1971) *Pioneer Work with Maladjusted Children: A Study of the Development of Therapeutic Education*. London: Staples Press.

Cooper, P. (1993) *Effective Schools for Disaffected Children: Integration and Segregation*. London/New York: Routledge.

Cooper, P. (1997) 'Valuing children: the important message of nurture groups', *Emotional and Behavioural Difficulties* **2**(3).

Cooper, P. and Lovey, J. (1999) 'Early intervention in emotional and behavioural difficulties: the role of nurture groups', *European Journal of Special Educational Needs Education* **14**(2): 122–31.

Cooper, P. and McIntyre, D. (1996) *Effective Teaching and Learning: Teachers' and Students' Perceptions*. Buckingham/Philadelphia: Open University.

Cooper, P., Arnold, R. and Boyd, E. (1999) *The Nature and Distribution of Nurture Groups in England and Wales*. School of Education, University of Cambridge.

Davie, R. (1994) 'A consortium for children: analysis of the dialogue with policymakers leading to the 1993 Education Act and the 1994 Code of Practice', *Therapeutic Care and Education* **3**(3): 206–12.

Davie, R., Butler, N. and Goldstein, H. (1972) *From Birth to Seven: A Report of the National Child Development Study*. London: Longman.

Department for Education (1992) *Her Majesty's Inspectors' Report for 1991–2*, para 79. London: DfE.

Department for Education (1994a) *Pupil Behaviour and Discipline*. Circular No. 8/94. London: DfE.

Department for Education (1994b) *The Education of Children with Emotional and Behavioural Difficulties*. Circular 9/94. London: DfE.

Department for Education (1994c) *The Code of Practice on the Identification and Assessment of Special Educational Needs*. London: HMSO.

Department for Education and Employment (1997a) *Excellence in Schools*. London: The Stationery Office.

Department for Education and Employment (1997b) *Excellence for All Children: Meeting Special Educational Needs*. London: The Stationery Office.

Department for Education and Employment (1998) *Meeting Special Educational Needs: A Programme of Action*. London: DfEE.

Department for Education and Employment (1999) *Social Inclusion: Pupil Support*. Circular 10/99. London: DfEE.

Department of Education and Science (1978) *Special Educational Needs. Report of the Committee of Enquiry into the Education of Handicapped Children and Young People* (The Warnock Report). London: HMSO.

Department of Education and Science (1989) *Discipline in Schools* (The Elton Report). London: HMSO.

Department of Health (1992) *Choosing with Care. Report of the Committee of Inquiry into the Selection, Development and Management of Staff in Children's Homes* (The Warner Report). London: HMSO.

Dunn, J. (1988) *The Beginnings of Social Understanding*. Oxford: Blackwell.

Dunn, J. (1995) 'Connections between emotion and understanding in development'. In *Cognition and Emotion*. 1995 special issue. Hove: Lawrence Erlbaum Associates.

Enfield Department of Education (2000) *The Nurture Group Curriculum*. Available from AWCEBD.

Feuerstein, R. (1969) *The Instrumental Enrichment Method: An Outline of Theory and Technique*. Jerusalem: HWCRI.

Forfar and Arneil (1992) *Textbook of Paediatrics*, 4th edn, ed. Campbell, O.G.M. and McKintosh, N., pp. 537–42. Edinburgh: Churchill-Livingstone.

Goldberg, S., Muir, R. and Kerr, J. (eds) (1995) *Attachment Theory: Social, Developmental, and Clinical Perspectives*. Hillsdale, NJ: The Analytic Press.

Gould, S.J. (1981) *The Mis-measurement of Man*. London: Norton.

Greenfield, S. (1997) *The Human Brain. A Guided Tour*. London: Weidenfeld & Nicolson.

Greenhalgh, P. (1994) *Emotional Growth and Learning*. London: Routledge.

Groothues *et al.* (1998) 'The outcome of adoptions from Romania: predictors of parental satisfaction', *Adoption and Fostering* **22**(4), 1998–99.

Harlow, H.F. and Harlow, H.K. (1972) 'The affectional systems'. In A. Schrier *et al.*, *Behaviour of Non-human Primates*, Vol. 2. New York: Academic Press.

Harris-Hendriks, J. and Figueroa, J. (1995) *Black in White: the Caribbean Child in the UK Home*. London: Pitman.

Hearnshaw, L.S. (1979) *Cyril Burt, Psychologist*. London: Hodder & Stoughton.

Henson, S. (1994) 'Nurture groups as a resource for children with special educational needs', M.Sc. dissertation, unpublished. London: Tavistock Institute.

Herrnstein, R.J. and Murray, C. (1994) *The Bell Curve. Intelligence and Class Structure in American Life*. New York: The Free Press.

Holmes, E. (1980) 'Educational intervention for pre-school children in day or residential care', *Therapeutic Education* **8**(2): 7.

Holmes, E. (1982) 'The effectiveness of educational intervention for pre-school children in day or residential care', *New Growth* **2**(1): 17–30.

Humphreys, M. (1994) *Empty Cradles*. London: Corgi.

Inner London Education Authority (1985) *Educational Opportunities for All? Report of the Fish Committee*. London: ILEA.

Iszatt, J. and Wasilewska T. (1997) 'Nurture groups: an early intervention model enabling vulnerable children with emotional and behavioural difficulties to integrate successfully into school', *Educational and Child Psychology* **14**(3).

Jackson, M. (1999) 'Nurture group news', *AWCEBD Newsletter*, Summer.

Jaffey, D. (1990) 'An evaluation of the work of nurture groups: an analysis of teacher and child verbal interaction in the nurture group and mainstream classroom'. M.Sc thesis, unpublished. Tavistock Clinic, London and Brunel University.

Johnson, B. (1996) 'Violent, man and boy', *Guardian*, 13 February, 6–7.

Lorenz, K. (1952) *King Solomon's Ring*. London: Methuen.

Lucas, S. (1999) 'The nurturing school', *Emotional and Behavioural Difficulties* **4**(3).

Maines, B. and Robinson, G. (1991) *Teacher Talk*. Bristol: Lame Duck Enterprises.

National Curriculum Council (1989) *A Curriculum for All*. Curriculum Guidance 2. York: NCC.

O'Connor, T.G. *et al.* (1999) 'Attachment disturbances and disorders in children exposed to early severe deprivation', *Infant Mental Health Journal*, Michigan Association for Infant Mental Health.

OFSTED (1995) *Carterhatch Infant School, Enfield. School Number 308/2011.* London: DfEE.

Panter, S. (1999) 'Nurture group news', *AWCEBD Newsletter*, Winter.

Parsons, C. *et al.* (1994) *Excluding Primary School Children.* London: Family Policy Studies Centre.

Pye, J. (1988) *Invisible Children.* Oxford: Oxford University Press.

Robertson, I. (1999) *Mind Sculpture.* London: Bantam Press.

Rutter, M. (1980) *Maternal Deprivation Reassessed*, 2nd edn. London: Penguin.

Rutter, M. and Smith, D. (1995) *Psychosocial Disorders in Young People: Time Trends and Their Causes.* Chichester: Wiley.

Rutter, M. *et al.* (1975) 'Attainment and adjustment in two geographical areas: 1.The prevalence of psychiatric disorder', *British Journal of Psychiatry* **126**: 493–509.

Rutter, M. *et al.* (1979) *Fifteen Thousand Hours: Secondary Schools and Their Effects on Children.* London: Open Books.

Rutter, M. *et al.* (1998) Developmental catch-up, and deficit, following adoption after severe global early privation', *J. Child Psychol. Psychiat.* **39**(4): 465–76

Rutter, M. *et al.* (1999) 'Quasi-autistic patterns following severe early global privation', *J. Child Psychol. Psychiat.* **40**(4): 537–49.

Rutter, M., Tizard, J. and Whitmore, K. (1970) *Education, Health and Behaviour.* London: Longman.

Saunders, P. (1996) *Unequal but Fair?* London: Institute of Economic Affairs.

Sereny, G. (1999) *Cries Unheard*, 2nd edn. London: Papermac.

Sylva, K. (1994) 'Findings and recommendations'. Ch. 8 in Ball, C., *Start Right: The Importance of Early Learning.* London: RSA.

Sylva, K. and Ilsley, J. (1992) 'The High/Scope approach to working with young children', *Early Education*, Spring.

Sylva, K. *et al.* (1986) *Monitoring the High/Scope Training Programme, 1984–5.* London: VOLCUF.

Thornton, M. (1994) 'Legislation and education'. In *The National Curriculum and Pupils with EBD.* Maidstone: AWCEBD.

Tizard, J. (1973) 'Maladjusted children and the child guidance service', *London Educational Review* **2**(2): 22–37, reprinted in Barnes, P. *et al.* (1984) *Personality, Development and Learning.* London: Hodder & Stoughton.

Tizard, B. and Hughes, M. (1984) *Young Children Learning: Talking and Thinking at Home and at School.* London: Fontana.

Underwood, J.E.A. (1955) *Report of the Committee on Maladjusted Children.* London: HMSO.

Vernon, P.E. (1969) *Intelligence and Cultural Environment.* London: Methuen.

Vygotsky, L.S. (1978) *Mind in Society.* Cambridge, Mass: Harvard University Press.

Woolfson, R. (1993) 'Interview with Feuerstein/We must challenge children', *Nursery World*, 26 August.

Yell, M. *et al.* (1999) 'Violence in American schools', *Emotional and Behavioural Difficulties* **4**(1).

Index